FROM PALM BEACH TO SHANGRI LA

FROM PALM BEACH TO SHANGRI LA

THE ARCHITECTURE OF MARION SIMS WYETH

JANE S. DAY
FOREWORD BY EUGENE PANDULA

PRESERVATION
FOUNDATION
OF PALM BEACH

RIZZOLI
NEW YORK

New York Paris London Milan

First published in the United States of America in 2021 by
RIZZOLI INTERNATIONAL PUBLICATIONS, INC.
300 Park Avenue South, New York, NY 10010
www.rizzoliusa.com

Publisher: Charles Miers
Editor: Douglas Curran
Production Manager: Alyn Evans
Managing Editor: Lynn Scrabis

Designed by Abigail Sturges

Printed and bound in China

2021 2022 2023 2024 2025/ 10 9 8 7 6 5 4 3 2 1

ISBN-13: 978-0-8478-6665-6
Library of Congress Control Number: 2021937768

Visit us online:
Facebook.com/RizzoliNewYork
Twitter: @Rizzoli_Books
Instagram.com/RizzoliBooks
Pinterest.com/RizzoliBooks
Youtube.com/user/RizzoliNY
Issuu.com/Rizzoli

CONTENTS

PREFACE

F*rom Palm Beach to Shangri La: The Architecture of Marion Sims Wyeth* is a celebration. On one hand, it is a long overdue monograph on the work of one of Palm Beach's most important twentieth-century architects. It touches on Wyeth's designs from his arrival in Palm Beach in 1919 until his death in 1982. Although it was impossible to include all of Wyeth's many projects, important examples of his work from Palm Beach, Florida, to Honolulu, Hawaii, are highlighted. This book is also a testament to the importance of historic preservation, particularly in an era when the built environment is often forfeited to developmental pressure. Without the forward-thinking pioneers of the preservation movement in Palm Beach many of the buildings depicted in this book would have been lost.

One of those pioneers was the late Robert I. Ballinger, Jr. an early chairman of the Landmarks Commission whose name is honored each year when the Preservation Foundation awards the prestigious Ballinger Award to an outstanding restoration project. When applicable, the Ballinger Award, Palm Beach Landmark Designation and listings in the National Register of Historic Places are noted at the end of each chapter as a way to emphasize and promote these critical programs.

This book is also an example of the ongoing work of the Preservation Foundation of Palm Beach. Their commitment to explore and document the rich history of the town is well known, but it must be emphasized that this mission can only be accomplished with the generous support of their many members, trustees and the Executive Committee. We thank them all. Advocacy, educational programs and publications like this one, which is based on an important collection of architectural drawings in the Preservation Foundation archives, help maintain the history of Palm Beach for everyone to enjoy. The hard work of putting together a book of this scope could only have been accomplished with the help of the Preservation Foundation staff under the leadership of President Amanda Skier.

We also owe a deep debt of gratitude to the Grande Benefactors of this work: Betsy and Paul Shiverick. Without their support, encouragement and "in the field" work as historic preservationists this book would not have been possible.

Cielito Lindo was featured on the cover of *Arts & Decoration* in 1928. The New York based magazine was published from 1910 until 1942.

Arts & Decoration

The Modern Note in Home Building and Decorating—Theatre, Music, Books

"Cielito Lindo"—The Home of Mr. and Mrs. James P. Donahue at Palm Beach   Marion Sims Wyeth, Architect

ARTS & DECORATION PUBLISHING CO. Inc.
PUBLISHER — ELTINGE F. WARNER
New York — Paris - London

JULY, 1928   PRICE: 50 CENTS

11

FOREWORD
EUGENE PANDULA

Publications celebrating important projects by accomplished architects, presented primarily as a photographic catalog of completed work, are ubiquitous. Less conspicuous are offerings that demonstrate the accommodation of elements such as time, budget, limitations of construction, personality, and politics that are necessary to bring a project forward. Rare is a work that also, at its core, searches for, finds and exposes the human characteristics and interactions ultimately involved in producing the architecture we experience. *From Palm Beach to Shangri La: The Architecture of Marion Sims Wyeth* is one of the rare books that introduce us to an extraordinary body of architectural achievement through the lens of personal relationship.

In many ways the architectural examples presented can and will speak for themselves. The quality of design, the choice of style, the nuance of siting, and the rigor of detailing are all self-evident. The means, methods and materials used in constructing these buildings are generally typical of the time period. It is the background narratives that allow us to understand the dynamic so important to the crafting of these projects and how, in fact, they contributed to the formation of community.

For those of us lucky enough to experience the work of Marion Sims Wyeth in person, there will be a greater understanding and appreciation of the built environment he contributed to and the necessary efforts to protect it. Individual buildings

will have more meaning, streetscapes will be more honored, and the way forward will be more considered. For others not yet familiar with Mr. Wyeth, this is the perfect introduction to a very important architect, his life's work, and its long-lasting impact on the place he made his home and far beyond.

Dr. Jane Day is a mentor, colleague and friend of three decades. For her, as a historian and scholar with both limitless curiosity and intellectual integrity, this project has been a labor of love from its inception. Determined to not produce the typical architectural monograph, the journey to find, obtain, and fit together pieces of this puzzle has been interesting to say the least. This is an effort to reveal rather than ignore or omit. It allows us to experience the challenges and opportunities of the time and consider some of the things that made Marion Sims Wyeth the architect he was. Jane has mastered not only an understanding of the complexities of creating architecture in context, but also the mostly hidden elements that can be major influences. In this presentation, she reveals those sometimes-contradictory elements in a genteel, positive, and constructive manner.

Marion Sims Wyeth could not have selected a more appropriate representative to provide us all the opportunity to witness his work. We are richer for Jane's efforts.

Study for the main approach to Greenfield, the home of Doris Duke's half-brother Walter Patterson Inman, in Georgetown, South Carolina, 1935.

13

INTRODUCTION

B y all accounts the architect Marion Sims Wyeth (1889–1982) was successful, hard-working, and well liked by his professional peers and many clients. With a remarkable commission list of over seven hundred projects he not only designed many new single-family homes and commercial buildings in Palm Beach but over the years altered and added to existing buildings. Important Wyeth projects are scattered all over Florida, from the Governor's Mansion in Tallahassee to Jacksonville, Coral Gables, Boca Raton, and the Seminole Golf Club in Juno Beach. He designed buildings in West Palm Beach including both Good Samaritan Hospital and the Norton Gallery and School of Art. Further afield you can see more buildings in Princeton, New Jersey; Georgetown, South Carolina; Scranton, Pennsylvania; New York City; and one spectacular mansion in Honolulu, Hawaii. Closer to home in Palm Beach Wyeth's designs are scattered in nearly every neighborhood on the island.

When I was asked by the Preservation Foundation of Palm Beach to compile a book on Wyeth's work, I was pleased but also felt a heavy responsibility. Having served as the Preservation Consultant to the Landmarks Commission of the Town of Palm Beach for twenty-one years I was familiar with many of the local structures Wyeth designed. I had written and defended designation reports, reviewed alterations to his historic structures, and given lectures about Wyeth's contributions to local architectural history. In Palm Beach Wyeth's name is well known and he has always been considered one of the "Big Five." These are the twentieth-century architects who in the early years of the resort's history developed what is now called the Palm Beach style, admired for its beauty and elegance as well as its extravagance. These men included Addison Mizner, John L. Volk, Maurice Fatio, Howard Major, and of course, Marion Sims Wyeth. But as well known as Wyeth has been locally, he has never really been given his due. Until now, there was no published book about the man or an in-depth study of his contributions to the world of architectural history.

With such a big challenge in front of me, I began by reviewing Town of Palm Beach landmarked structures. This was a start, but how do you pull together a long life and a career of over fifty-four years and still make the story interesting? How do you sort through a vast commission list of over seven hundred projects and decide what to include? Secondary sources are plentiful but sometimes contain inaccuracies and repeat polite but vacant platitudes. Writing about architecture is also a difficult task. Beyond the description of stylistic features, a writer hopes to help the

Marion Sims Wyeth, circa 1940.

14

15

16

reader envision the space and scale of a building that would be better experienced on location in real time.

To get closer to the truth about any architect and his career, I felt as a historian that I must return to the primary sources: the architectural plans and the buildings themselves. To study those documents the Robert M. Grace Library at the Preservation Foundation of Palm Beach is the place to begin. Founded in 1980 with a "goal to preserve the architectural history of Palm Beach and educate its residents about their heritage," the Preservation Foundation of Palm Beach is the caretaker of the library and two important collections, The Jack C. Massey Architectural Archives, and the Mr. and Mrs. Paul Van der Grift Architectural Image Collection. These resources contain over fifty thousand original architectural drawings, three thousand property files, and thousands of photographs, slides and digital images. They include the works of architects John L. Volk, Belford W. Shoumate, Henry K. Harding and Marion Sims Wyeth. The Wyeth collection was donated to the Preservation Foundation in 1993 by Sidney K. Neill. Neill had supervised Wyeth's projects in the Bahamas from 1937 to 1940 and after receiving his Florida architectural license in 1946 became associated with the firm Wyeth, King & Johnson until Wyeth retired in 1973. These drawings are an outstanding historical resource and were invaluable for this book.

I also believe it is important to look at architecture in context. To get a more accurate picture of Marion Sims Wyeth and his work, I had to consider the times when the buildings were constructed and investigate the clients who commissioned the projects. Some of the structures were built on speculation, like the houses for the Golf View Road Development Corporation. Some reflected the fantasies and strong personalities of such rich and powerful clients as Marjorie Merriweather Post and Doris Duke. Evidence shows that in architecture finances always have to be considered, especially in public projects like the Florida Governor's Mansion but, I also found that finances mattered to the wealthiest of owners. Where available I have incorporated anecdotes and cultural details into the story along with the aesthetic descriptions, hoping to make Wyeth's life and career come alive.

Finally, Marion Sims Wyeth was not only a talented architect but was also an active member of the Palm Beach community. In civic affairs he volunteered his time at many of the important institutions that differentiate Palm Beach from surrounding communities. He was a member of the Civic Association, The Society of the Four Arts, Bethesda-by-the-Sea Episcopal Church and was appointed by local government to serve on the sometimes-controversial Town of Palm Beach Art Jury, a committee that reviewed local architectural projects for appropriateness and good taste. He was an early member of the legendary Everglades Club, The Bath and Tennis Club and the Seminole Golf Club. As an outdoorsman Wyeth loved to play tennis and golf, and was an enthusiastic fisherman. He was a dedicated family man, who with his wife Eleanor raised a son and three daughters in the small Palm Beach island community. He was liked by everyone.

This book was written with the deepest admiration and respect for Marion Sims Wyeth and his long and successful career. It does not attempt to cover all his work but instead discusses highlights that illustrate the breadth of his talent and scope of his varied architectural style. It is also a celebration of historic preservation as almost every building that is included in this book is locally landmarked or listed in the National Register of Historic Places. Palm Beach is a town of beauty and spectacular architecture built by a handful of talented men. Prominent among them was Marion Sims Wyeth: The Dean of Palm Beach Architects.

Wyeth at the drafting table.

FOLLOWING PAGES
The iconic Everglades Club opened in 1919 with great success.

CHAPTER ONE

A STRONG FOUNDATION

*Wyeth brought outstanding training and exposure to great architecture
to his new practice in the still underdeveloped Town of Palm Beach.*[1]

—Polly Anne Earl, Executive Director, Preservation Foundation
of Palm Beach from 1983–2004

Every architect knows the importance of a strong foundation. In the building trades the strength of a structure depends upon its underpinnings. Marion Sims Wyeth's successful career had just that kind of strong foundation based on the building blocks of a supportive family, a world class education, and tremendous talent. These beginnings along with a pleasant and likable demeanor helped him navigate a fifty-four-year architectural practice through the recurring cycles of economic booms, busts and wars that punctuated the twentieth century. Wyeth's designs moved easily from the Spanish and Mediterranean styles popular in the 1920s to the Georgian, Colonial and French Revival styles that were favored in mid-century. On a few occasions he explored Modernism. The common thread throughout all Wyeth's work was that it successfully adhered to his basic tenet of creating "quiet, subdued and rational buildings."[2]

Marion Sims Wyeth was born on February 18, 1889, in New York City into a well-educated family of medical professionals. He was named in honor of his maternal grandfather J. Marion Sims (1813–1883), a physician who is often called the "Father of Gynecology" and served as the head surgeon at the Women's Hospital of the State of New York. John Allan Wyeth (1843–1922), Marion Sims Wyeth's father, was born in Alabama, studied at the University of Louisville in Kentucky and later at the Bellevue Hospital Medical College in New York. He got his surgical training in Paris studying with his future father-in-law who had relocated to France during the American Civil War. In 1886, John Allan Wyeth married his mentor's daughter, Florence Nightingale Sims who became Marion's mother. John Allen Wyeth founded the first post-graduate medical school in the United States, New York Polyclinic Graduate Medical School and Hospital which later merged with the Columbia University College of Physicians and Surgeons. Both father and grandfather served terms as the President of the American Medical Association.[3]

The young Marion Sims Wyeth and his family lived at 19 West 35th Street in New York City in the building where his father practiced medicine. They summered in Winter Harbor, Maine, at the Grindstone Inn. Wyeth went to the Morse & Rogers

Marion Sims Wyeth (left) and his
partner Frederic Rhinelander King
(right) with their wives, Eleanor Orr
Wyeth and Edith Morgan King, at
the Beaux-Arts Ball, New York City.

20

School where headmaster I. L. Rogers, gave a recommendation for his application to the Lawrenceville School in New Jersey writing, "We have found him always ready to do all work which was given to him and do it well. He is stronger on the classical than on the mathematical side and his English work has been very good."[4] Wyeth attended Lawrenceville for two years, graduating in 1906. His roommate was George Orr, whose sister would later become Wyeth's wife. Then it was on to Princeton University for four years. In 1910, he obtained an A.B. (Bachelor of Arts) degree. At Princeton, Wyeth was a member of the Ivy Club and an editor of the *Princeton Tiger*, the second oldest college humor magazine in the country. A Princeton Alumni Weekly later recollected that Wyeth "excelled at tennis and the study of architecture which would wield him great influence over the next sixty years."[5]

Finishing his undergraduate studies, young Wyeth decided on a professional career in architecture and headed to Paris, France. There he enrolled in the architecture school at the prestigious École des Beaux-Arts where he won a number of prizes. He received his diploma in 1914. But academics were not the only advantage given to a young student in Paris. Wyeth wrote, "When I was at the Beaux-Arts, I used to go down to Italy and my aunt had a villa." He noted that while in Europe he met Rudyard Kipling and Auguste Rodin, and was friendly with Lawrence Grant White, the son of the famous American architect Sanford White. Most important for his career, he met his lifelong friend and future business partner, architect Frederic Rhinelander King (1887–1972).[6]

World War I began in 1914, but instead of going back to the United States Wyeth traveled south to Rome. His father was a supporter of President Woodrow Wilson and had arranged a job for Marion as private secretary to Thomas Nelson Page, the American ambassador in Italy. Largely an honorary position that would allow Wyeth to study classical architecture in the field, the year presented other valuable lessons. When Wyeth arrived in Rome in October 1914, he moved into a pensioni "for economy" and although he wrote that it was a comfortable place, he was "rather lonely." At Christmas the young man was excited about the embassy Christmas party. Ambassador Page gave him a gold knife and Mrs. Page presented him with a new umbrella. At a holiday party at the British Embassy on December 28, Marion was so charming that the Pages asked him to move into the American Embassy. "A great day this, as I have been miserable and lonely. The Pages are too kind," Wyeth wrote. A severe earthquake hit the town of Avezzano in central Italy on January 13, 1915, causing over 30,000 deaths and millions of dollars in damages. Along with two other young men, Wyeth was sent to the disaster area to inspect damages and distribute blankets and supplies. Wyeth also made sketches and wrote down architectural proportions of what remained.[7] These real-world life experiences with exposure to classical architecture, unexpected challenges, and sophisticated international society would serve the young architect well, especially when he moved to Palm Beach and had to interact with the new American aristocracy.

Before Wyeth launched his career in Palm Beach, there were a few other milestones to complete. On his return to the United States, he first entered the architectural offices of Bertram G. Goodhue and then Carrère and Hastings where he learned the intricacies of the Spanish Revival style that had been popularized in the Panama-California Exposition of 1915 in San Diego, California. Marion noted in a later interview, "I started at $15 a week as a draftsman and finally $30 and then $45. In November of 1915, he married Eleanor Noyes Orr, the sister of his Lawrenceville roommate.[9] When the United States entered World War I on April 6, 1917, Wyeth was shipped out to Europe and served in the army air corps building aero plane hangars in England. At the end of the war, he returned to the United States and took his young family to Florida to see a house he had worked on as a draftsman. "Finding that there were no established architects in the vicinity of Palm Beach, I decided to make it my home."[10]

On February 1, 1919, when Wyeth arrived in Florida much of the natural landscape was scrub pine and wilderness. Early Palm Beach was largely a hotel resort centered in a small area around the Royal Poinciana and Breakers hotels. Visitors arrived by train to enjoy the short social season that extended from New Year's

Eve until Washington's Birthday. As people got a taste of the beautiful subtropical winter weather in south Florida, they became eager to find a place of their own and extend their stay. World War I was over, the economy was good and building opportunities abounded. The Florida Land Boom was on.

Wyeth was the second architect to open an office in Palm Beach. Addison Cairns Mizner (1872–1933), who was largely self-taught, arrived in January 1918 with his friend Paris Singer, son and heir to the Singer Sewing Machine fortune. Mizner made a splash with his big personality and fanciful designs for the Everglades Club and Worth Avenue. He popularized Mediterranean Revival architecture and put his stamp on the style of the entire resort. Then came Marion Sims Wyeth. Unlike Mizner, Wyeth arrived with a wife, two small daughters and a portfolio of academic degrees and prestigious apprenticeships. Mizner offered the newcomer a job in his own office which might have been the safe path, but Wyeth declined. Wyeth's credentials were impeccable. All he needed was a break.

The opportunity came almost immediately. Wyeth had already secured one job for a house on Brazilian Avenue in Palm Beach. Then with the help of his father's medical connections, Marion received the first major commission of his career for the construction of the new Good Samaritan Hospital in West Palm Beach. The *Palm Beach Post* reported that Marion was "particularly suited for the commission, as he is the son of the famous New York surgeon Professor Wyeth, of the Polyclinic Hospital."[11] Up until that point, the only medical care in the area around Lake Worth was in a small wood cottage with five patient beds. Palm Beach visitors and local residents alike had been fundraising for a new hospital since 1914. And in perfect synchronicity with a country on the cusp of the Roaring Twenties, the fundraisers were spectacles. There were tea dances and dinners and masquerades. Society pages reported on a "Ziegfeld Frolics" party at the Embassy Club (now the Society of the Four Arts) where there was a Charleston dance contest and ringside tables cost $1000. In 1920, the biggest social event of the season was the Washington's Birthday Ball at the Royal Poinciana Hotel. Four thousand people were reported to have attended and all proceeds went to the new hospital. "The dining room," the *Palm Beach Daily News* reported, "was decorated like Mount Vernon's garden. Everyone at some time during the evening or into the early morning hours took a wheelchair ride along the lake trail or into the jungle. Many wheeled over to Bradley's to join the throng at his casino or have some of the famous Welsh rarebit or bacon and eggs."[12]

Good Samaritan Hospital was built in 1921 in the Spanish Revival style with only thirty-five beds.

When the fundraising was complete Wyeth built a two-story, thirty-five-bed hospital in the Spanish Revival style with arches, pedimented windows, a prominent parapet and a screen door at the entrance. There were four doctors, and men and women's wards were partitioned by curtains. There were a few private rooms. It was a great improvement from the old cottage. Within a year, however, the hospital was congested, and charity patients had to be placed on cots in the hallways. Wyeth continued to work on hospital additions and improvements throughout his career. In 1921, Wyeth designed the Delphine Dodge Isolation Hospital, which was paid for by a generous donation from automobile manufacturer Horace Dodge and named for his daughter. Horace Dodge later died from a complication of the Spanish Flu after spending weeks in his room at the Breakers Hotel because there was no hospital to treat him in the area. The building later became the maternity ward and pediatric unit.[13]

Besides the institutional work, in 1920 Wyeth forged ahead with upscale single-family home designs. Frank H. Clement, a retired railroad contractor from Niagara Falls, New York, bought twenty-seven acres for $175,000 and created El Bravo Park, a large section that stretched from the ocean to Lake Worth just south of the Everglades Club. Clement completed all the infrastructure and subdivided the land into thirty-six lots. He hired Wyeth to design the first house, hoping to attract buyers. The public liked what they saw, and Wyeth received commissions for a dozen other houses in the subdivision over the next few years. The young architect was on his way to success. Although the original El Bravo house was later expanded by Addison Mizner for stockbroker John F. Harris with the addition of a Medieval tower and named El Castillo, it still stands as a Landmark of the Town of Palm Beach and won the prestigious Ballinger award in 2009.[14]

In 1927, Addison Mizner added a crenellated tower to Wyeth's simple 1920 design in El Bravo Park. The house was renamed El Castillo.

FOLLOWING PAGES
Wyeth's 1920 living room for Frank Clement retains the herringbone style flooring, fireplace, and stenciled ceiling, giving the room timeless charm.

CHAPTER TWO

HOGARCITO

… I was walking down Golf View Road towards the Everglades parking lot, and Martin Sweeney, then manager of the newly opened Everglades Club introduced me to a very attractive couple, Mr. and Mrs. Edward F. Hutton, who were looking over a possible site for a cottage they wished to build.[1]

—Marion Sims Wyeth

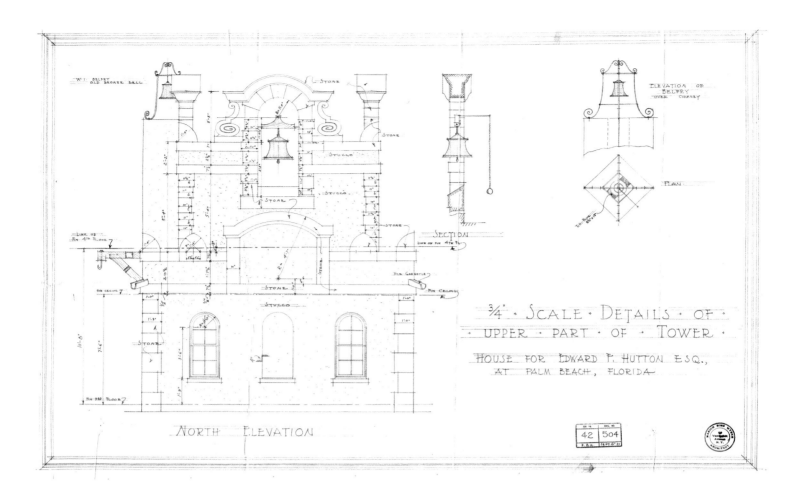

NORTH ELEVATION

³⁄₄" · SCALE · DETAILS · OF ·
· UPPER · PART · OF · TOWER ·

HOUSE FOR EDWARD F. HUTTON ESQ.,
AT PALM BEACH, FLORIDA

B y 1921, the Florida building boom was well underway, and the Town of Palm Beach was thriving. In 1916, the Ocean Road (A1A) had been blacktopped and opened, attracting motorists to the island rather than just those who arrived by boat or train. The Everglades Club, developed by Paris Singer and designed by architect Addison Mizner, had opened on January 25, 1919, with twenty-five charter members and was a rousing success. This Mediterranean Revival–style building not only changed the architectural essence of the resort but moved the social scene away from Henry Flagler's hotels in the northern part of town, south into an exclusive private realm centered on Mizner's new Everglades Club complex and its companion streetscape, Worth Avenue.

Marion Sims Wyeth, who opened his Palm Beach office in 1919, had already completed a number of important commissions in both Palm Beach and West Palm Beach. His chance introduction to newlyweds Marjorie and E. F. Hutton on that spring day was the beginning of a friendship that would last throughout his career and give him the opportunity to work on two of his most significant residential projects, Hogarcito and Mar-a-Lago. It also gave him the opportunity to work with a blank slate and lay out the style and ambience of Golf View Road.

Marjorie and Edward Hutton were part of a new and younger social scene that was developing in Palm Beach the Roaring Twenties. They had each been married before. Marjorie had been divorced, which was still considered scandalous, and "Ned" was a widower whose wife had died in the 1918 Spanish Flu pandemic. They both had children. Marjorie had vacationed in Palm Beach for more than a decade prior to her marriage to Hutton, but now as a newly married couple, the pair was considered stylish and trendy. They were invited everywhere.

One of four Spanish mission-style bells that graced the tower, circa 1922.

Marjorie Merriweather Post had inherited her father's Postum Cereal Company which would eventually become General Foods, and E. F. Hutton was a financier of renown, who had opened brokerage offices in New York and Palm Beach. Besides socializing with local aristocrats, they also mingled with a new group of artistic and noteworthy friends, Florenz Ziegfeld, the producer of New York's Ziegfeld Follies, and his wife actress Billie Burke, who went on to play Glenda the "Good Witch" in the film *The Wizard of Oz*. The Huttons participated in activities at the Everglades Club and swam at the Breakers Hotel. They went to balls and private parties. They frequented the gambling casino at E. R. Bradley's Beach Club. Mrs. Eva Stotesbury, the acknowledged Grande Dame of the Palm Beach winter resort who had given Addison Mizner one of his first large residential commissions, took Marjorie under her wing. As Nancy Rubin related in her biography, *American Empress: The Life and Times of Marjorie Merriweather Post*, after World War I, "being 'smart' and 'sassy' replaced being 'proper' and 'respectful'...."[2] Mrs. Hutton was both smart and sassy.

The Huttons spent the winter season of 1920–21 renting one of the maisonettes, or small apartments, at the Everglades Club, and Marjorie was not happy. According to a later interview, she said that "the apartment was so horribly noisy on both sides of it that we just couldn't cope."[3] The couple started looking for a lot to build a house where they could find some quiet and entertain during the short Palm Beach social season. They didn't have far to go.

When Paris Singer, a son of Isaac Singer who founded the Singer Sewing Machine Company, bought the land for the Everglades Club in 1918, he purchased a plot that went from Lake Worth to the Atlantic Ocean, and from Peruvian Avenue on the north, south to El Bravo Road. On their search for a piece of

land to build their new vacation home, the Huttons just walked down the street from their maisonette at the Everglades Club, had their serendipitous introduction to architect Marion Sims Wyeth, and bought the first lot on a completely undeveloped street named Golf View Road.

Hogarcito, as the new house was called, means "little home," but the house that was built was not really modest by anyone's standards but Marjorie's. And the lot they had chosen on the Everglades Club golf course was spectacular. The footprint of the house was an asymmetrical U-shaped Spanish Revival design and it featured a prominent four-story Mission-style bell tower. The *Palm Beach Post* took notice that there were "three bells facing north, east and west, running from the center arches [of the tower], and a fourth bell of bronze hangs framed with wrought iron directly over the chimney. Each bell is a different tone and when rung simultaneously, the effect produced is that of bells of a quaint mission."[4]

When viewing the house from the street, the four-story bell tower is the main focus. The eye is drawn upwards from the front door to the curvilinear parapet just below the bells by a prominent tiled panel. These tiles are repeated around

FACING PAGE
Railings in the stair hall match the original.

ABOVE
The circular stairs on the upper landing led to staff rooms and then onto the roof of the bell tower.

33

The original living room, circa 1922.

FACING PAGE
Decorative tiles representing the story of Don Quixote surround the fireplace in E. F. Hutton's office.

FOLLOWING PAGES
LEFT
Marjorie Merriweather Post Hutton (in the dark hat) and her daughters enjoy Hogarcito's yard overlooking the Everglades Club golf course, circa 1922.

RIGHT
One of the original paintings on the walls of the dining room.

the front door and again around the French doors and arched fanlight that float above the entrance with a small cantilevered wrought iron balcony. Wrought iron lanterns that flank the French doors are also set in tile. The tower is edged with quoins and divided into increasingly smaller sections by a series of raised stucco belt courses. The effect adds a strong vertical element to the overall design and makes the bell tower the most important feature on the front facade. For the Huttons, Wyeth had stripped the prevailing Mediterranean Revival style of much of its ornamental excess and simplified the house into an excellent example of the California Mission style, focusing on the American colonial precedent of Spanish Revival architecture rather than the European model. The original cost was reported to be $35,000.[5]

After their first winter in the Golf View Road house, the Huttons asked Marion Sims Wyeth to design an addition to the original structure. Marjorie's "little home," was indeed proving too small for her entertaining needs. The addition included a new master bedroom suite, a double car garage with a turntable so that the cars would never have to back out onto Golf View Road, and various improvements to the gardens and décor. Everything was scheduled to be completed by January 10, 1924, when the Huttons were to arrive in Palm Beach from New York.

Correspondence between Ed Hutton and Marion Wyeth during the construction of the Hogarcito addition reveals details about the working relationship and growing friendship between the two men. It also shows the influence Mrs. Hutton had on the purse strings. Earlier letters between the architect and client, written when the original house was being constructed, were formal in both greetings and salutations. By 1923, when the addition was being put on, they were addressing each other more affectionately as "My dear Marion," and "My dear Ed." On September 27, 1923, when discussing driveway material in conjunction with the new garage, Hutton wrote, "Mrs. Hutton has asked me to explain to you that a cheaper form of roadway for the garage is quite the thing to consider. In other words, you suggested cement instead of brick. Cement being cheaper, I would say put it in."[6] On October 4, 1923, Hutton again wrote to Marion about the telephone Mrs. Hutton wanted in her bathroom, approving the added expense. "Regarding the telephone installation—that is ok. And that is about all there is to it. So, shoot the works."[7] If Marjorie wanted a telephone in the bathroom, she would have it.

We also learn from the correspondence between Hutton and Wyeth what it was like to live in the houses of the 1920s before the invention of air conditioning. Hutton wrote:

> I would appreciate it very much if you would put a ventilator over the door going out on to the porch, so that I can get some ventilation or a draft through from the window outside the porch. As it is now the room is very warm when the wind is from any direction other than the ocean, so just give me a ventilator that I can work with a little iron rod, pushing it up and down.[8]

As construction of the addition was nearing completion, Wyeth wrote to Hutton on December 22, 1923, just three days before Christmas. He wanted to wrap up the final details of the job, but also had a favor to ask:

> As the disbursements on the Palm Beach house to date total forty-nine thousand eight hundred twenty-three and 94/100 dollars ($49,823.84) I am enclosing my professional bill for architectural services in the amount of Two thousand dollars ($2000.00) which will bring your payments to me up to Forty-five hundred dollars ($4500.00).... I am sending you this bill at this time as it is going to be a lean Christmas at my house unless I can raise some money. [9]

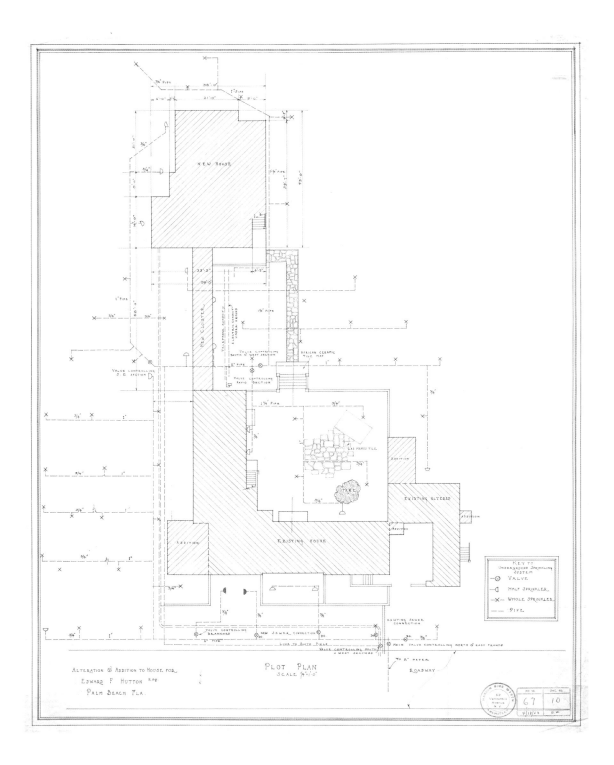

PLOT PLAN
SCALE ⅛"=1'0"

ALTERATION & ADDITION TO HOUSE FOR
EDWARD F HUTTON ESQ
PALM BEACH FLA.

FACING PAGE
Marjorie Merriweather Post Hutton with her daughters Eleanor Post Close and Adelaide Breevort Close, circa 1922.

FOLLOWING PAGES
The view across the modern swimming pool to the cloister that connects the 1921 house on the left and the 1923 addition on the right.

This one paragraph shows a rare vulnerability on the part of Wyeth regarding his financial situation at the end of 1923. It also shows the trust Wyeth had in Hutton to honor the request in a timely manner. In the end, the bill was paid and the friendship between Marion Sims Wyeth and E. F. Hutton deepened.

Hogarcito was an architectural success. The *Palm Beach Daily News* called it "one of the most desirable properties on the Palm Beach island." But despite its beauty, the house was still too small for Marjorie. When the E. F. Huttons moved on to Mar-a-Lago, the property on Golf View Road was sold to Edward's brother Franklyn Hutton and his daughter Barbara Hutton, the granddaughter on her mother's side of Frank W. Woolworth, the founder of the Woolworth Five-and-Ten-Cent Stores. Today the house is a Landmark of the Town of Palm Beach, gracing the northern edge of the Everglades Club golf course between the 1st tee and the 3rd green, just as it did in 1921.

CHAPTER THREE

THE GOLF VIEW ROAD DEVELOPMENT COMPANY

I am a bull on Palm Beach…

—E. F. Hutton[1]

n 1922, while planning an addition to Hogarcito, Marjorie Post Hutton wanted to ensure that her neighbors on Golf View Road were the "right kind of young marrieds." One way to accomplish this, she felt, was to control the size and style of other homes in the neighborhood. With this in mind, a partnership was formed called the Golf View Road Development Company. Using land from Paris Singer's Ocean and Lake Realty Development Company, fifteen lots were plotted along the north side of the empty street just east of the Everglades Club and two further lots, besides Hogarcito, were carved out on the south side into the golf course. Marion Sims Wyeth was chosen as the president and architect of the company, and his working partner was builder Harry Raymond Corman, a master builder from Nebraska who was known for his ability to solve difficult problems associated with construction. E. F. Hutton financed the entire project but insisted on remaining a silent partner. Before he accepted any individual private commissions on the street, Marion Sims Wyeth planned and designed five houses to be built on speculation. He acted as the real estate agent and set up an office and model in one of the houses to promote sales, reporting back to Hutton, who had bankrolled the construction, on progress and each prospective purchaser.

As a young architect in Palm Beach, Wyeth had been presented with a tremendous opportunity and an enviable blank slate for his architectural creations. He chose to use the popular Mediterranean Revival style for the neighborhood, pulling details from Spanish, Italian and Moorish architecture. Every house was unique. The five L-shaped houses were built on the north side of the street on alternating lots thus providing an opportunity for future property owners to expand their homes or add extensive gardens. Service into the garages at the rear of the structures was through an alleyway that separates Golf View Road from the more commercial district on Worth Avenue. Swimming pools, if they were desired were to be built in the front yard. The plan was innovative and original. Golf View Road is today one of the most beautiful streets in

El Azulejo

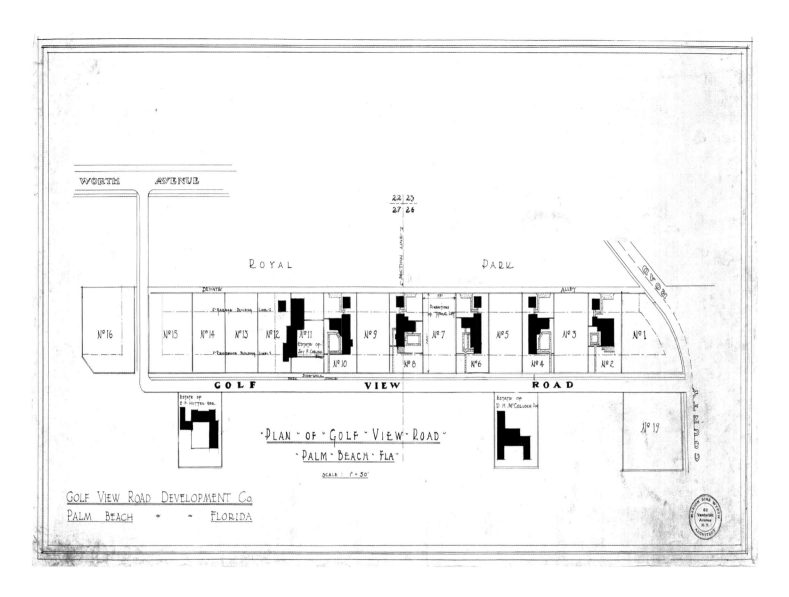

Palm Beach and the location makes it easily walkable to the Everglades Club, Worth Avenue, and the beach. These houses are also good examples of Wyeth's talent because they are a collection of his thoughts and designs that were developed on speculation with no owner input. The streetscape is Wyeth's vision. It was a wonderful opportunity, but even with E. F. Hutton's backing, finances were a worry from the beginning.

In a letter dated June 26, 1922, Wyeth wrote to Hutton from New York, "I am leaving tomorrow for Palm Beach and hope to have everything lined up for our construction project. I talked to Mr. Tompkins [Hutton's attorney] over the phone and if it should be necessary for me to call on you for money before he completes the papers, I will wire the same." Wyeth also noted, "The market in building materials has been going up and I have had to take the bull by the horns and order a certain amount of building tile and lumber without waiting for the papers to be signed. This I may have to pay for while I am down there." As a personal note at the end of the typed letter Wyeth wrote in his own hand, "I would have come to see you before leaving but unfortunately have been in bed for a week—sort of a nervous breakdown."[2] Marion Sims Wyeth felt pressured to make a success of the Golf View Road Development Company and his young career.

Later that June, Hutton deposited a draft of $10,000 for Wyeth to begin. Both men seemed anxious and by October 30, 1922, Hutton was writing to Wyeth, "Have you had any nibbles, and have you written to some of the people who have shown interest? I think there is a possible chance with Jim Donahue, also Charles McCann. Do not mention my name, however, in this connection. I have no doubt it will be sold, so do not get discouraged. Keep me posted."[3]

50

By December 19, 1922, nothing had sold, and costs had gotten out of hand. Hutton wrote to his bookkeeper, Mrs. Jaffa, who sent the checks to Palm Beach. "Honor the drafts. I cannot stop at this stage so will have to see it through to completion."[4] That same day Hutton wrote to Wyeth expressing his displeasure. "I am somewhat disappointed to learn that we cannot complete the situation on the amount agreed upon…." He added another paragraph worrying about how the Golf View Road construction might impact his stay at Hogarcito that season. "I wish to suggest, in regard to the construction of the houses, that you try, as far as possible, to have those completed thoroughly which are near our house, so that when we arrive on the 15th of January we will not be bothered with workmen directly opposite." Hutton finished the letter with a reprimand, "I will be disappointed if some of the houses are not placed before the end of the season…. If you start the ball rolling the rest will go quickly, but the first two or three purchasers we have got to find."[5]

Two days before Christmas, on December 23, 1922, Wyeth wrote back clarifying his cost increases. Wyeth explained, "In addition to the cost of the building operation, we had allowed $1000 per house for planting and here I have really run into trouble. All the property was considerably under the level of the street and I have been forced to carry sand all summer to raise lots above water. This alone has cost $5000 and my planting has had to be done in excess of that."[6] The prices of the houses started at $35,000 but by December Wyeth told Hutton that in January he would have to raise the prices to $37,000. He also assured him that the houses closest to Hogarcito would be finished first.

Houses started to sell after January 1923. In April, The *Palm Beach Post* commented that "Mr. Wyeth's row of five $35,000 houses on Golf View Road … has set a fashion for houses of real distinction, appropriate to people of quite moderate means."[7] Three sold immediately and the other two were leased. Wyeth sailed for Spain in June 1923 "for fresh inspiration for his work."[8]

A year later on January 28, 1924, E. F. Hutton wrote affectionately to Marion Sims Wyeth. "My dear Wyeth … I note house number four has been sold…." He went on, "I note that you have decided to boost the price of the remaining house to $45,000. I hope you get it, but if some boy comes along and flips $41,000 or $42,000 at you, don't let it get away from you. After the remaining house is sold, and our books are clear, we will look around for something else. I am a bull on Palm Beach, and when this is sold, we can make other plans for going ahead."[9]

In the end, all five of the houses built on speculation sold, and the Golf View Road Development Company was a success. The press described the street as having a row of Spanish homes of dignity for the discerning gentleman.[10] Today six of the development's eight original houses by Marion Sims Wyeth, including four of the homes that were built on speculation, have been designated as landmarks of the Town of Palm Beach. The four remaining spec houses are:

EL AZULEJO – 6 GOLF VIEW ROAD

El Azulejo was one of the first model houses of the Golf View Road Development Company to be sold. Named for a form of glazed ceramic tilework first introduced into Spain and Portugal by the Moors during the thirteenth century, the Arabic root of the house's name literally means "a small polished stone." The purchasers were Mr. and Mrs. Charles E. F. McCann, whom Hutton had cultivated in 1922. McCann was an attorney from Manhattan and Oyster Bay, New York. His wife, Helena, was the oldest daughter of F. W. Woolworth of the Woolworth Five-and-Ten-Cent Stores. Taking advantage of Wyeth's idea to build on alternate lots so that purchasers could expand their homes as needed, the McCanns did just that. They bought the lot next door, and between 1924 and 1929 added a number of additions including a fifty-by-twenty-five-foot living room that extended to the east. The McCanns had three children: Frazier, Helena and Constance. Helena was presented at the Court of St. James in London in 1931 with her cousin Barbara Hutton, who after 1927 wintered in Palm Beach just down the street at Hogarcito.[11]

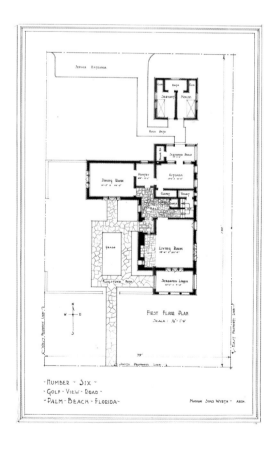

51

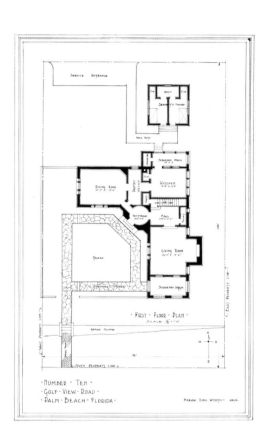

CASA LA BELLA – 10 GOLF VIEW ROAD

Mr. and Mrs. George H. Nicolai of Detroit, Michigan and Great Neck, Long Island, started coming to Palm Beach in 1905. Originally, they stayed at the Breakers Hotel. They purchased their home on Golf View Road, the third of the spec houses to sell in 1923, and became fulltime residents of Palm Beach in 1938. Mr. Nicolai had started in the brokerage business in Milwaukee, Wisconsin, and moved to Detroit, where he owned the *Detroit Free Press* with Edward Stair. Later he became a silent partner in the Stair and Havlin Theatrical Management Syndicate that operated a large chain of theaters from the East Coast to Kansas City. Additions and renovations to the house were completed throughout the years. Wyeth added an open loggia to the house in 1928. When Mr. Nicolai passed away in 1945, Marion Sims Wyeth, who had become a friend as well as the architect of record for his house, served as an honorary pallbearer.[12]

In 1956, while completing a renovation project for the second owners, Lester Napier Stockard and his family, architect John L. Volk enclosed Wyeth's loggia and removed a large stone medallion from above the front door. Mr. Stockard was in the shipping business.

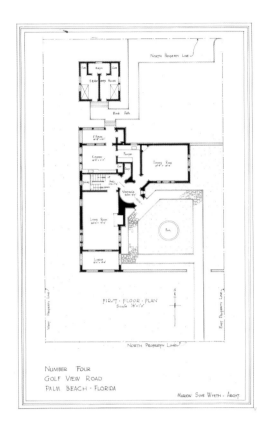

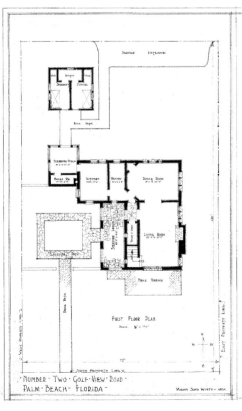

4 GOLF VIEW ROAD

In 1925, Archibald McNeil, Jr. bought 4 Golf View Road, one of the two remaining spec houses. His family had long ties to Palm Beach. His parents had taken a train from Connecticut to Palm Beach to attend the opening of the Royal Poinciana Hotel in 1892. They were friendly with Henry Flagler and visited seasonally. Mr. McNeil, Jr. was a state senator in Connecticut where he published daily newspapers in Bridgeport and worked alongside his father in the Archibald McNeil & Sons Company, a wholesale coal dealership. The family were supporters of the Democratic Party and entertained the likes of William Jennings Bryan, Woodrow Wilson and Franklin Delano Roosevelt in their homes in Connecticut and New York. Living in Palm Beach during the boom times of the 1920s, Archibald McNeil, Jr. became interested in real estate speculation and joined the ill-fated Mizner Development Corp in Boca Raton, Florida, serving as director of publicity and advertising. The firm went bankrupt in 1926.

The house at 4 Golf View Road has changed over the years. An original rooftop garden on the northwest section of the house has been enclosed and a sunroom and bath addition were completed in 1968. In 1970, a swimming pool was added. More space was needed and a second story addition and guest house in the rear of the property in 2006.

CASA MARIANA – 2 GOLF VIEW ROAD

Rich in Mediterranean Revival–style details, Casa Mariana was the last of the Golf View Road Development Company houses to sell. The front door faces the front walkway and has a small balcony above the entrance with seashell styled capitals. An exterior staircase with risers from Addison Mizner's Los Manos Potteries dominated the southwest elevation and led to a rooftop garden. A real estate advertisement from 1925, printed when the original lease had expired and the property was put on the market for sale, extols the uniqueness of the house and the view:

> This is the only house on Golf View Road available at this time. The view from the little observation tower on the roof is alone worth the price of the house. One can see the entire Everglades Golf Course, Lake Worth, and the Ocean.[13]

The house was named for Marion, the wife of owner John N. Steele, an attorney and copper financier who bought the property in 1925.

CHAPTER FOUR

LA CLARIDAD

*Mrs. Clarence Geist has had plans made for the construction
of a handsome new residence on Golf View Road opposite
the residence of Mr. Edward F. Hutton.*[1]

—*The Philadelphia Inquirer,* March 30, 1924

Two houses stand across the street from each other at the western terminus of Golf View Road, a small private street just east of Palm Beach's exclusive Everglades Club. Both houses were designed by architect Marion Sims Wyeth, one in 1921 and one in 1924. Both designs fit into the broad general architectural category called the Mediterranean Revival style that has many variations and was so popular during the 1920s. But that is where the similarity stops. The existing houses are quite different. One is simple, based on the American colonial precedent on Spanish Revival architecture sometimes called the California Mission style and the other is ornate with all the grandeur and high style of the Spanish Baroque. The contrast might have been due to Wyeth's growing experience or perhaps his inspiring trip to Spain in 1923. More likely the different background and temperament of the houses' owners, E. F. Hutton and Clarence Geist, two self-made men, played the biggest role.

Born in 1866 on a farm in La Porte, Indiana, Clarence Geist initially traveled to the American West where he bought and sold livestock. He was there for a few years until he returned to Chicago because, as he later recalled, "no one in the West had any money, and I discovered the fact that I could not make money where there wasn't any."[2] By all accounts, Geist was a hard worker and took a job as a brakeman on the Rock Island Railroad. He sold real estate for a time. Then a chance encounter and unlikely friendship with Charles Dawes, who would later serve as the vice president of the United States under Calvin Coolidge, presented an opportunity that would change Geist's life and lead him into a prosperous future. Attorneys and politicians, Charles Dawes and his brother Rufus were active in the utilities business. When an opportunity arose in Hammond, Indiana, to develop a gas company, Geist

Clarence Geist

FACING PAGE
Wyeth's final house
on Golf View Road was
designed in 1924 in the
Spanish Baroque style.

was sent ahead to broaden the customer base so that the business would increase in value. Geist went door to door selling kitchen ranges from the back of a wagon, creating a larger subscriber base. Under the tutelage of the Dawes brothers, he also learned the inside workings of the utilities industry. Eventually, Geist bought a small company, which he later sold to the Philadelphia United Gas and Improvement Company.[3] Money started flowing in.

With new prospects in hand, Geist moved to Philadelphia and in 1905 married Florence Hewitt. He started the Philadelphia Suburban Water Company which supplied water to forty-nine towns near the city. This asset was later expanded to become the C. H. Geist Company, operating public utilities throughout the area. An enthusiastic golfer, he also founded the Seaview Golf Club in Atlantic City, New Jersey, after reportedly being rejected at the Ocean View Country Club, which catered to the area's blue bloods. Geist was flamboyant and showy, a big tipper who liked to make an entrance and be noticed. Some people found him coarse, but his nephew, Bradley Geist, related that he was a funny, delightful man, and "generous to a fault."[4]

Clarence and Florence Geist started coming to Palm Beach with their family as early as 1916. In 1922 they spent the season at the Royal Poinciana Hotel. By 1924, they had made the commitment to build a winter home and hired Marion Sims Wyeth to design a house for them just down the street from the Everglades Club, where Geist was a member and a friend of founder Paris Singer. The architecture of the house—called La Claridad, meaning *clarity*— reflected Geist's style and personality. The result was the most ornate house Wyeth completed on Golf View Road.

Two prominent elements stand out when you look at the south facade of La Claridad, the front entrance and the three-story tower on the western corner. The wooden double doors at the front entrance are surrounded by staggered quoins and reached by ascending stone steps. The whole element is crowned with a low-relief sculpture that contains shields of heraldry, pilasters and a garland border. A casement window with more quoins is centered above. This Plateresque design of intricate and complicated detail harkens back to Baroque Spain and is based on ornate patterns often found on silver plate.

The fenestration on the tower is centered on that element and proceeds upward. It begins on the ground floor with casement windows separated by pilasters and capped with a pecky cypress beam. Above a pair of French doors, quoins and a stone balcony hang over the street below, as if waiting for someone to appear and give an audience to the public. The stone shield above the doors extends up into the space of the double belt course, drawing your eye to three casement

windows joined by stone arches and framed with pilasters at the top of the tower. The tower element has a hip roof covered with Cuban tile while the rest of the house has a gable roof. Wrought iron grills with the monogram "CG," for Clarence Geist, decorate some of the first-floor windows. Shutters, fanlights over French doors, and stone sills were all used on the original house in a complex pattern of excess and luxury.

Marion Sims Wyeth pulled out all the stops and applied a full set of historic Spanish architectural details onto Clarence Geist's vacation home. An article in the *Palm Beach Post* on April 4, 1925, raved about the authenticity of the interior design as well. "This house which occupies a commanding position where Golfview road turns on its way to the sea, is said to be one of the most beautifully furnished of the period houses in Palm Beach and Mr. Geist had a representative scouring Spain all last summer for beautiful things to place in it."[5] In 1925, Clarence Geist was one of many wealthy industrialists wintering in Palm Beach, enjoying his golf game and impressive new home.

By 1927, the real estate boom in Florida had come to a halt. Where others saw failure, Geist saw opportunity and actively pursued the challenge of taking over the bankrupt interests of the Mizner Development Corporation in Boca Raton, a small town twenty-six miles south of Palm Beach. As a former board member of Mizner's company, Geist knew what he was getting. When looked at with hindsight, the Mizner Development Corporation's project in Boca Raton was doomed from the start. Built on speculation and leveraged land sales, Addison Mizner's dream was underfinanced. When the Florida banks failed in 1926, Mizner looked elsewhere for funding while continuing to advertise a fantasy he could never deliver. The money did not materialize. Some of Mizner's buildings, including the hotel called the Cloister Inn and the Administration Building, were complete, but there was still much to do to produce a fully functional winter resort. The horrific hurricane of 1926 that devastated south Florida put the final nail in the coffin of Addison Mizner's Boca Raton dream.

Reports from July 1927, when the bankruptcy of the Mizner Development Corporation was adjudicated, stated that one hundred and seventy-three creditors were left with $4,192,000 in unsecured debt. Three years later, they received .001 percent

Graceful steps rise to the wooden Spanish-style paneled door which is surrounded by quoins.

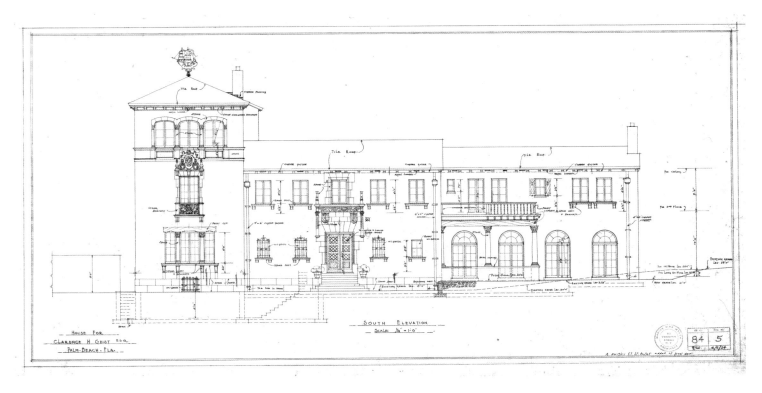

63

FACING PAGE
Stairs led to the terrace in the private
courtyard.

ABOVE
A cantilevered stone balcony supported
by scroll brackets with a relief sculpture
above dominates the tower.

on their claims.[6] By October 1927, Clarence Geist had put in a silent bid to buy the assets in Boca Raton and was successful in his efforts. Figures vary as to his complete investment, but most accounts conclude that it was a seven-million-dollar deal with an immediate payment of "$71,000 cash and the assumption of all mortgages and obligations."[7] Geist's strategy was to forge ahead and improve the original concept of Mizner's plan based on his successful New Jersey hotel and club. His first order of business was to expand the Cloister Inn by adding three hundred rooms. He hired the architectural firm Schultze and Weaver, who were well-known hotel

The Tackbary Residence,
Boca Raton, Florida, 1930.

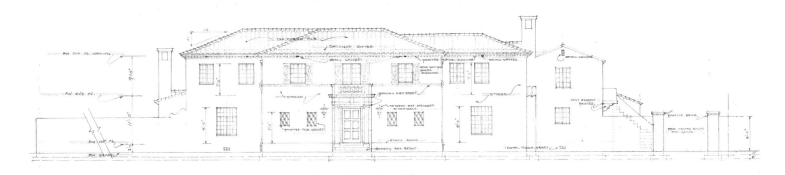

NORTH ELEVATION

builders and had completed other important projects, including the Biltmore Hotel in Coral Gables, the Breakers in Palm Beach, and the Waldorf-Astoria in New York City. The expanded property opened in late 1929. Clarence Geist leased La Claridad in Palm Beach and moved with his family into a suite at the new Boca Raton Club in January 1930.

The Palm Court at the Boca Raton Club was adjacent to the Cathedral Dining Room. It was demolished in 2021.

Work on the Boca Raton Club continued, and Marion Sims Wyeth added his architectural skill to the project. Pleased with Marion's work on La Caridad, Geist, like E. F. Hutton before him, did not hesitate to hire Wyeth again. Soon after the opening of the new resort it was apparent that Mizner's original lounge needed to be enlarged for the increased number of guests. There was also a dance terrace just outside Schultze and Weaver's cathedral dining room that was open to the night air and needed protection from evening breezes coming in from the water. Architectural historian Donald Curl, an expert on both Addison Mizner and Boca Raton, wrote about Wyeth's work. "The addition to the lounge extended out over the lake, and numerous engineering drawings showed its steel piling support, though the architectural details of the extension matched Mizner's original design."[8] The new cloister that Wyeth designed to protect the dance floor picked up on elements used by both Mizner and Schultze and Weaver but added Wyeth's classical touch. Glazed Gothic arches faced Lake Boca on the outside of the cloister to protect guests from the elements while seven rounded arches supported by cast stone columns opened inward, inviting couples onto the dance floor on warm winter evenings.

Geist continued with general improvements. The Boca Raton inlet to the Atlantic Ocean was dredged and the bulkhead around the lake to the east of the hotel reinforced. Cabanas were built on the beach and a bridge was constructed over the Intracoastal Waterway to get to them. A new train station was added on Dixie Highway so that Geist could travel directly to Boca Raton instead of stopping in Palm Beach. True to a utility magnate's first priority, the Town of Boca Raton got a new water treatment plant, which was said to be the best in the area.

In 1947 the house was divided at the end of this hallway. The historic living room at the end of the hall is now next door.

RIGHT
The entry hall has an arched ceiling and original tile floor.

The staircase in an historic
image from 1924 and today.

72

The dining room in the 1924
house (left) became the living
room (above) when the house
was divided in 1947. The herring-
bone-style tile floor, cypress
ceiling and fireplace have all been
restored.

Clarence Geist plated the land remaining outside of the boundaries of the club and formed the Spanish River Land Company, so he could sell lots and build houses on speculation in hopes of restarting the local real estate business. Marion Sims Wyeth was hired to complete two of the houses. Built on Camino Real, the wide boulevard immediately south of the club's entrance, they are identified in Wyeth's archive as House # 6 and House #7 for the Spanish River Land Company. On September 9, 1930, the Fort Lauderdale paper announced that they were to be in the Spanish style and would cost $45,000 each.[9] Much more simple and classical in detail than Wyeth's work for Clarence Geist at La Claridad, House #6, which is now known as the Tackbary Residence (see page 66), was landmarked in 1991 by the City of Boca Raton. It has a front entrance centered on the main block of the two-story house with a classical quarry keystone surround. Painted tile grills add interest on the first floor. Windows are casement and a truncated hip roof with Cuban tiles tops the design. House # 7 has been demolished.

La Claridad stayed in the Geist family into the 1930s, although they were rarely in residence. Clarence died in 1938 and, under new ownership, in 1948 the house was divided into two single-family homes. Belford Shoumate was the architect for James Hannah, the new owner of the east side of the property. Both sections of La Claridad are now landmarks of the Town of Palm Beach, celebrating Clarence Geist's entrepreneurship and Marion Sims Wyeth's architectural expertise.

A new addition to the home adds rooms for twenty-first century livability.

FOLLOWING PAGES
A swimming pool adds charm to the west patio.

CHAPTER FIVE

MAR-A-LAGO

It isn't my taste. It's the taste of Joe Urban. I don't want anyone to think I was the architect in charge.

—Marion Sims Wyeth[1]

The front gate at Mar-a-Lago is covered with antique Spanish tiles and flanked by figures of medieval page boys holding lights.

The first-floor cloister is a transitional space between the living room and outdoor patio. The walls are covered in tiles and capitals are carved with birds and acanthus leaves.

ar-a-Lago is arguably the most recognizable house in Palm Beach. You can see its massive seventy-five-foot tower with red tiled roof from both South Ocean Boulevard (A1A) in Palm Beach and across Lake Worth in West Palm Beach. When you drive across the Southern Boulevard Bridge to Palm Beach and turn left heading north you catch a glimpse of the east lawn and the large single paned glass window that frames the view from inside the loggia to the Atlantic Ocean. To approach the house, you drive under an arched gate that is covered with fifteenth-century Spanish tiles and flanked by figures of medieval page boys holding torches. From there it is a short drive west, through an alley of palm trees, to the porte-cochère and the entrance. Everywhere you look there are carved stone sculptures and gilded wooden elements. The ornamentation and details are overwhelming. It is grand. It is flamboyant. It is over the top. It is the epitome of the excess of the Florida real estate boom of the 1920s. And it is not what Marion Sims Wyeth, the classically trained Princeton graduate, imagined when he started working on the project with Marjorie Merriweather Post and her second husband E. F. Hutton.

Although Wyeth worked well with the Huttons on Hogarcito, their first Palm Beach house on Golf View Road, and completed a substantial addition a year later, everyone was well aware that their original "little home" was too small for Marjorie Merriweather Post Hutton and her ambitions as a social hostess. For the new project she wanted something grand and from the start took a hands-on approach. With her real estate agent Lytle Hull and armed with a geological survey that identified the most solid ground on the island of Palm Beach, Mrs. Hutton crawled through the underbrush herself as she searched for the perfect site for the new house. The search began south of Worth Avenue

PAGES 82-83
Austrian Franz Barwig and his son Walter created many of the sculptures on the property from Doria stone shipped from Genoa. Italy. This detail is at the porte-cochère.

PAGES 84-85
The upper cloister gives access to guest rooms and secretaries' offices. It is covered with a mission-style shed roof with prominent outriggers of carved gilded eagles. The seventy-five-foot tower is beyond.

in an area that at the time was largely overgrown with lush vegetation and subtropical jungle. The property she finally chose had five hundred feet of ocean frontage. It covered 16.98 acres and stretched from the Atlantic Ocean to Lake Worth all the way across Palm Beach island. By consulting the geological survey Marjorie thought practically as well as aesthetically. She knew if she could anchor the new structure with concrete and steel to the coral rock that formed the substratum of the land, the house would be sturdy enough to withstand tropical storms and hurricanes. Envisioning her new home, secured and centered in the middle of this large plot of land with sweeping views to both the ocean and Lake Worth, Marjorie named the house Mar-a-Lago, literally "sea to lake."[2]

With the site purchased for a reported $500,000, Marjorie again asked Marion Sims Wyeth to design her new home.[3] Wyeth remembered, "She came to my office and we developed a plan which embodied her own ideas and featured the elliptical patio and cloister which is incorporated in the present house."[4] Later Marjorie

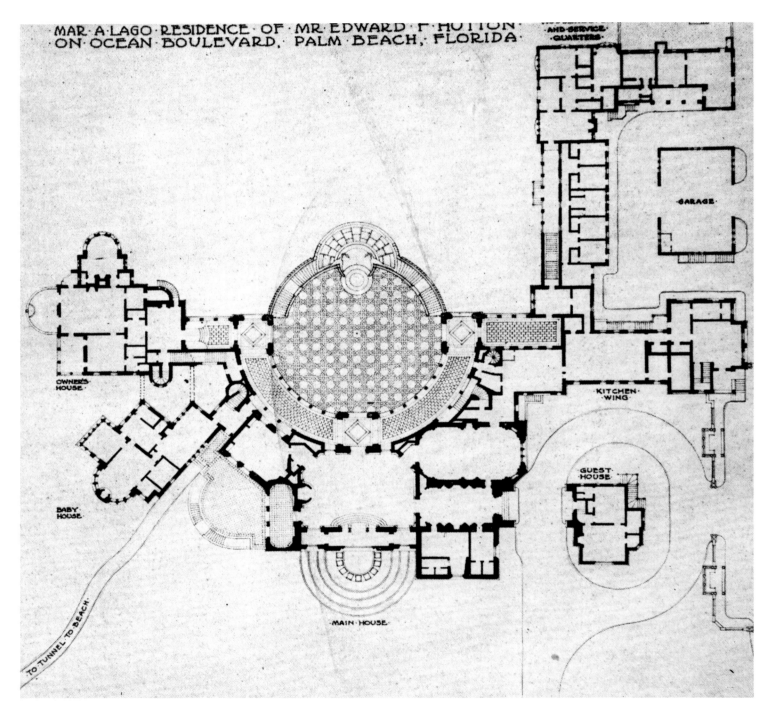

MAR·A·LAGO·RESIDENCE·OF·MR·EDWARD·F·HUTTON· ON·OCEAN·BOULEVARD, PALM·BEACH, FLORIDA·

The pavilion Wyeth added in 1961 was the site of Mrs. Post's square dances.

stated that "her thought was that a Florida house could be constructed with the background idea of [a] camp, namely a main building and different guest rooms and family rooms [that] would be connected with a patio."[5] Wyeth worked on the plans over the winter of 1924–25. On May 2, 1925, the *Palm Beach Post* reported that the plans were coming along. Landscaping had begun and fourteen of the largest cabbage palms in Palm Beach were planted along the ocean front. "It was expected," the paper noted, "that Mrs. Hutton will return to Palm Beach about the first of June to look after the landscaping and consult with the architects."[6] That is when everything changed.

Although the interior floor plans were progressing, Marjorie was unclear about what she wanted for the exterior design and was unhappy with Wyeth's conservative and classical suggestions. She wanted something innovative that would differentiate her house from other palatial mansions that were being built in Palm Beach during the 1920s. She did not want to hire Addison Mizner, the "society architect" favored by many seasonal residents. She did not know where to turn but the answer appeared in an unlikely spot. While on a fishing trip in the Florida Keys with her husband and good friends Florenz Ziegfeld, the Broadway producer, and his wife, actress Billie Burke, the design of the new house was discussed. Ziegfeld suggested that she talk to Joseph Urban, a Viennese architect and set designer who had worked for Ziegfeld and designed scenery for his Ziegfeld Follies. Marjorie was intrigued. Marion Sims Wyeth was left in the dark until Ed Hutton sent word that

Aerial view before beach cabanas
were added to form the Mar-a-Lago
Beach Club in 2002.

The Huttons, Old Westbury,
Long Island, 1933.

89

they would like to meet with him in Palm Beach while sailing their 202-foot, three-masted schooner *Hussar* from Jacksonville to Miami.[7]

Just getting to Hutton's boat required some effort for Marion Sims Wyeth and his wife, Eleanor. The *Hussar* was too large to navigate the Palm Beach Inlet and enter Lake Worth, so Marion chartered a small boat and headed out to sea. "Ed and Marjorie were on deck to greet us as we came alongside," wrote Wyeth. It was then that he met the other guests and finally "last but not least Flo Ziegfeld and his scene painter and decorator, Joseph Urban."[8] The boat dropped anchor off Gus's Baths which was at the head of Worth Avenue and the party climbed into a tender to come ashore at the pier. From there they all headed to Wyeth's house Tre Fontane on Middle Road for lunch. After lunch, Marjorie, Urban and Wyeth drove to Wyeth's office to review the portion of the plans that had already been finished. Joseph Urban took the plans with him and the Huttons returned to their boat and sailed on to Miami.

After this informal meeting, the Huttons kept Wyeth on as one of the architects on the Mar-a-Lago project, but forced an association with Joseph Urban that made Marion uncomfortable. An undated handwritten note to Hutton reads: "Dear Ed. The enclosed missive from me to you is to cover the business end of the Hutton-Wyeth-Urban Triangle. If you want me to explain anything please phone me." The attached formal typed letter to Ed Hutton dated June 19, 1925, clarifies the situation. "Having done business with you for the past five years, without any agreement in writing, I cannot bring myself to draw up a formal contract between ourselves, but in view of the fact that Mr. Urban and I are associated together, for the first time, I think it advisable for the protection at all parties...."[9] This information is remarkable. It shows that Marion Sims Wyeth and Edward F. Hutton completed both Hogarcito and the Golf View Road Development Company on the basis of a handshake and mutual respect. Now with a third party involved on Mar-a-Lago, Wyeth suggested, and Hutton agreed, to draw up a formal contract based on the Standard Form of Agreement between Owner and Architect, published by the American Institute of Architects. The fee for the two architects' services was to be 15 percent (instead of Wyeth's usual 10 percent fee) on all drawings, drafting, keeping of accounts and general administration and supervision. A separate contact was drawn up for the builder.

Contracts were not the only challenges. One incident almost halted the construction of Mar-a-Lago. In March 1926, Cooper Lightbown, the town's major builder, was working on the foundation of Mar-a-Lago when Mrs. Horace Dodge, the widow of the automaker, sold her lot just south of the Huttons for $1,500,000. The new owners announced plans to build a twelve-story apartment building and to subdivide the rest of the land for retail and small residential development. Edward Hutton stopped work on Mar-a-Lago immediately, reporting that he "did not want to have his winter estate in such surroundings."[10] Work only resumed when a group of seasonal residents got together and purchased the land from the developer. Rather than turn the property into more residential units, they formed the exclusive Bath and Tennis Club and built one of the most iconic structures in Palm Beach.[11]

Meanwhile, Marion Wyeth heard little about Mar-a-Lago until May of 1926, almost a year after the boating rendezvous and the contract with the Huttons and Joseph Urban. Then, while in New York, Mrs. Hutton's decorator told him that Joe Urban was making working plans for a house for Mrs. Hutton in Palm Beach. "This was news to me," Wyeth wrote.[12] On May 10, Wyeth submitted a bill to Hutton for work he had completed before Urban was brought on board. This was for the Slat House and site preparation including moving Washington palms and coconut trees from Henry Flagler's White Hall south to the lot. He noted that it "would be unjust for me to charge you the fifteen percent (15%) fee on work that had been done by me prior to the association [with Urban]"[13] Reading between the lines it is clear that Wyeth was not happy collaborating with Urban. E. F. Hutton, however, is reported to have begged Wyeth, "You've got to come back on this job because Joe Urban may be an artist but he's not a practical man. He doesn't know

much about plumbing or heating or electricity or any of the basic things that go into a house."[14] Wyeth consented but the working relationship with Joe Urban was short lived. On September 10, 1926, Wyeth wrote to Hutton about the situation, "I am leaving for Florida September 25 to take a general survey of the condition of your building operation, and on my return I would like to have you consider my withdrawal from the work of associate architect, upon completing the shell of the building, i.e. before the interiors are done."[15]

Mar-a-Lago was completed a year later in January 1927. It had taken four years and six hundred laborers to build. The budget had reportedly gone from $1,000,000 to $2,5000,000. Wyeth later told an interviewer that Urban brought

Marjorie Merriweather Post with her daughter Dina Merrill and granddaughter Heather Robertson at Mar-a-Lago, 1960.

91

The most prominent features on the oceanfront facade are the tower and the great arched window with its deep border of carved griffins.

sculptor Franz Barwig and an army of stone cutters from Austria. "They pitched tents out on the lawn there. They worked there and slept there, and they carved by hand these Gothic-like gargoyles that are on the house to shed water and capitals on the columns. It was all done in the old early method of doing things."[16] The finished Mediterranean Revival estate with Hispano-Moresque details had one hundred and fifteen rooms, eight hundred windows and doors, forty-two bedrooms and thirty-one baths. Ed Hutton is reported to have remarked, "I wanted a seaside cottage and look what I got."

Although throughout the rest of his life Marion Sims Wyeth did his best to disown his part in the design of Mar-a-Lago, architectural historian Donald W. Curl made a good case that the layouts of both Hogarcito and Mar-a-Lago shared a common lineage. Curl saw both houses as a "series of pavilions that corresponded to different functions of the house."[17] Wyeth's purchase of a rare collection of fifteenth-century Spanish and Moorish tiles from the estate of Mrs. Horace Havemeyer at the beginning of the project also added an important element to the elaborate décor. It is said that with over thirty-six thousand tiles, they were eventually used to cover doors, arches and walls throughout the house and are one of the first things a visitor notices.[18] In the end, the bones of the structure, punctuated with the unique antique tiles were Wyeth's contribution. The exterior, decorating and fanciful elements were Joseph Urban's. But the entire estate was totally a reflection of Marjorie Merriweather Post and the opulent era in which she lived.

Wyeth stayed close with both Mr. and Mrs. Hutton. He worked with E. F. Hutton again designing the Seminole Golf Club in 1929, and in 1961–62 added a dance pavilion to Mar-a-Lago for Marjorie's famous square dances. The new pavilion had a stage for the orchestra, a projection booth and a motion picture screen. He also added two staff cottages to the northwest section of the property and did other maintenance on Mar-a-Lago.[19] By that time the Huttons had long been divorced and Marjorie had taken back her maiden name. Wyeth had moved from Middle Road to Woodbridge Road just north of Mar-a-Lago, making him a neighbor to the house he would not acknowledge. Marjorie Merriweather Post still enjoyed Wyeth's friendship and put a gate in her fence so that he could use the "pitch-and-putt" golf course on her property any time he wanted.

Marion Wyeth's final words on Mar-a-Lago are recorded in the article he wrote about his experience. "Mar-a-Lago is a notable architectural creation and deserves to be preserved in years to come as a symbol of grand old days now gone."[20] The estate is listed as a National Historic Landmark and is also protected by its designation as a local Palm Beach Landmark. Although Mrs. Post left the house to the Federal government upon her death in 1973, the upkeep proved too expensive for the government and Mar-a-Lago was returned to the estate. It was bought by Donald J. Trump in 1985 and at first used as his personal residence. In 1993, after extensive negotiations with the Town of Palm Beach the house was converted into the Mar-a-Lago Club. It served as the Winter White House for the 45th President of the United States, Donald J. Trump.

CHAPTER SIX

SEMINOLE GOLF CLUB

A one-word name spoken with the reverence of a sacred oath.[1]

—James Dodson, columnist for *Golf Magazine*

n March 31, 1929, six months before the stock market crash ushered the nation into the Great Depression, a new sporting facility was planned nine miles north of Palm Beach on one hundred and seventy acres of land in Juno Beach, Florida. The property had 2600 feet of ocean frontage and the club was scheduled to include an eighteen-hole golf course, swimming pool, tennis courts, clubhouse and cabanas on the beach. The cost was estimated to be $500,000. Edward F. Hutton was the president of the new club. Scotsman Donald Ross of Pinehurst, North Carolina, who had designed the Gulfstream Golf Club just south of Palm Beach, was chosen to design the layout of the course, and Marion Sims Wyeth, Hutton's architect for both Hogarcito and Mar-a-Lago, was hired to design the clubhouse and other facilities. The new club was named The Seminole Golf Club but in later years as the club's prestige grew, serious golfers like champions Ben Hogan and Arnold Palmer spoke of it with great affection and just called it Seminole.[2]

The idea to build Seminole came to E. F. Hutton while playing golf with Hunter Marston at the Gulfstream Golf Club fifteen miles south of Palm Beach. There was a waiting list for membership and the course seemed to always be crowded. Stuck behind an aging and slow-moving John Sanford, Hutton and Marston asked to go ahead and play through. Marston later recalled that Sanford snapped at him, "Hunter, you young snips make me mad. We old men put up all the money for this club, and you young snips want us to stay on the sidelines while you ride through. No, stay behind—in your turn."[3] Legend has it that at that moment the younger men looked at each other and decided to build their own course. Hutton told people that he wanted to build the finest golf club in the world.

A welcoming entry courtyard
at Seminole, circa 1930.

By 1929, Marion Sims Wyeth and E. F. Hutton had known each other for eight years. They had lived through the challenges of both Hogarcito and Mar-a-Lago, and successfully developed one of the finest streets in Palm Beach, Golf View Road. Hutton was said to be exceedingly fond of Wyeth. They were frequent golf companions and it came as no surprise that Wyeth was selected to be the architect for the new club. He was also invited to be one of the hundred and ten charter members, the only architect amongst a roster of Palm Beach's leading aristocrats that included names like Harold Vanderbilt, Barclay Warburton, Rodman Wanamaker, E. T. Stotesbury, Otto Kahn, Mortimer Schiff, and, of course, E. F. Hutton.[4]

As Donald Ross worked on the layout of a golf course that became widely praised, Wyeth drew up the architectural plans for the building. "In Spanish design, the clubhouse will be an attractive, but simple structure, the U-shaped building surrounding a large patio and swimming pool. There will be a basement above ground, and a large main floor, topped by servants' quarters and a sunroom. The exterior will be of stucco with ornamental concrete trim and will be tomato color."[5] The entrance, a huge pecky cypress door, was centered on the south facade of the main block of the building with a beautiful lacy wrought iron gate. The rounded arch of the door included a keystone in the center and was topped with a graceful sundial between two Seminole Indian Warriors, paying homage to the name of the club and Old Florida. Four windows at ground level surrounded with quoins hint at the above ground basement on the interior. Each window has a small balconette balanced on the top quoins with a wrought iron railing. Nestled under the eaves of the red-barrel tile roof, a ribbon of shuttered windows gives a lightness to the elegant symmetrical design.

PAGES 98-99
Sculpture of a Seminole Warrior
enhances the entry. It was cast by
Nicholas Koni in honor of Hunt T.
Dickinson, the club's sixth president,
and presented to the club's board of
directors in 1968.

PAGES 100-101
The west facade of the clubhouse
as seen from the golf course, circa
1930.

An early drawing shows that Wyeth
suggested the name of the club,
flanked by Seminole figures, be
placed above the entrance. Instead,
a sundial was positioned over the door.

Arnold Construction Company was the successful bidder for the contracting
work and completed the job in less than eight months. There was some trouble with
the swimming pool. Water continually seeped into the pool's construction pit. Then
the contractor caught a saltwater fish in the hole. Wyeth associate William Johnson
reported that after bringing in more pumps to keep the water out, they realized that
they had tapped into saltwater and would "never be able to pump the ocean dry."
The pool became saltwater rather than fresh, and the fish was mounted and hung
in the men's locker room.[6]

The Seminole locker room that Wyeth envisioned is said to be one of the most
loved and impressive in the country. "Wyeth's innovative design included a large
open and airy men's locker room with high cypress-beamed ceilings and simple
paneled lockers. Creating a vast but oddly intimate space that quickly came to
symbolize the casual elegance of the new club."[7] The *Palm Beach Post* reported just
before the opening that the men's locker room, which comprised the north wing of
the structure, was the main feature of the building. In an effort to keep the club as
a sport's center, rather than a social hub, there was no loggia.[8] Other spaces of the
building included a dining room and terrace that overlooked the swimming pool, a
card room, and a mile-long drive from Dixie Highway to the front door.

102

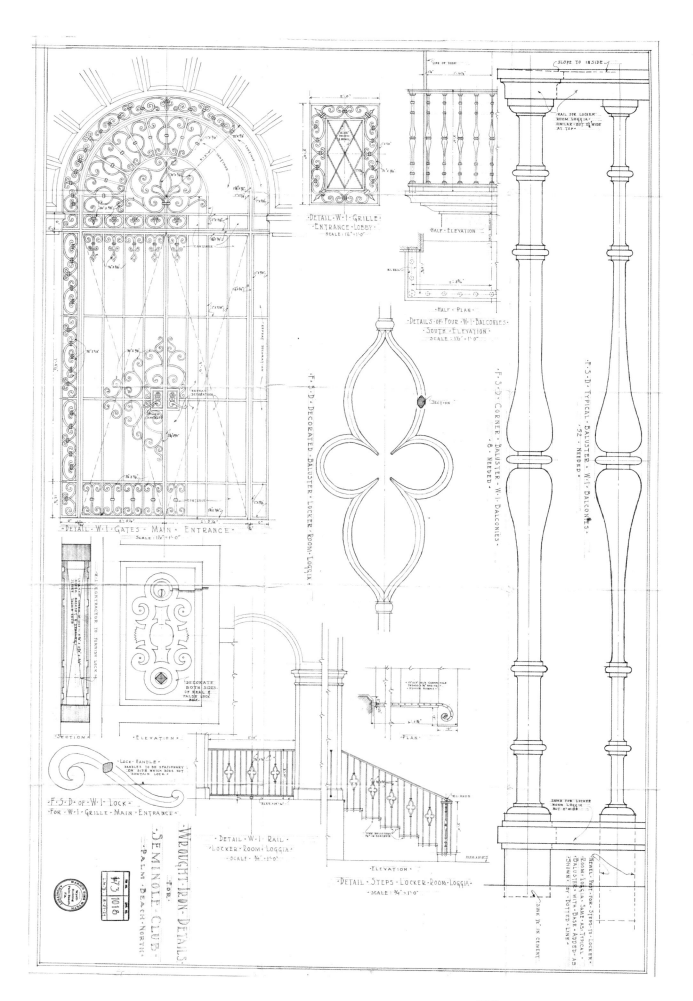

·DETAIL·W·I·GRILLE·
·ENTRANCE·LOBBY·
SCALE: 1½" = 1'-0"

·HALF·ELEVATION·

·HALF·PLAN·
·DETAILS·OF·FOUR·W·I·BALCONIES·
·SOUTH·ELEVATION·
SCALE: 1½" = 1'-0"

·SECTION·

·DETAIL·W·I·GATES·MAIN·ENTRANCE·
SCALE: 1½" = 1'-0"

·DECORATE·
·BOTH·SIDES·
·OF·NEWEL &·
·FALSE·LOCK·
·BOX·

·SECTION·

·ELEVATION·

·LOCK·HANDLE·
HANDLES·TO·BE·STATIONARY·
ON·SIDE·WHICH·DOES·NOT·
CONTAIN·LOCK·

·F·S·D·of·W·I·LOCK·
FOR·W·I·GRILLE·MAIN·ENTRANCE·

·DETAIL·W·I·RAIL·
·LOCKER·ROOM·LOGGIA·
·SCALE: ¾" = 1'-0"

·ELEVATION·

·PLAN·

·ELEVATION·

·DETAIL·STEPS·LOCKER·ROOM·LOGGIA·
·SCALE: ¾" = 1'-0"

·F·S·D·DECORATED·BALUSTER·LOCKER·ROOM·LOGGIA·

·F·S·D·CORNER·BALUSTER·W·I·BALCONIES·
·8·NEEDED·

·F·S·D·TYPICAL·BALUSTER·W·I·BALCONIES·
·52·NEEDED·

·WROUGHT·IRON·DETAILS·
·FOR·
·SEMINOLE·CLUB·
·PALM·BEACH·NORTH·

#73·1016

A portrait of E. F. Hutton,
completed in 1929 by F. C. Von
Hausen, hangs in the clubhouse.

BELOW AND FACING PAGE
Seminole's world-famous men's
locker room has a cypress beamed
ceiling and wooden lockers with
carved panel doors. The room is
sometimes referred to as "the best
four walls in golf."

In Seminole's original charter it stated that the club would be exclusively for men. But the rule was broken on opening day, January 1, 1930. The first person to tee up was Grace, the thirteen-year-old daughter of Charles Minot Amory. By April, Wyeth had a new commission. He was hired to add a thirty-five-by-twenty-five-foot women's lounge to the east of the building. By that time the architecture of the new building was also being praised in the press. "In Spanish farmhouse design, the clubhouse represents an interesting departure from the elaborate buildings that are prevalent in Palm Beach, combining simplicity and utility with a charming exterior."[9] Marion Sims Wyeth had used his classical training to get back to basics. E. F. Hutton had fulfilled a dream and built one of the finest golf clubs in the world. In 2020, *Golf Digest's* most recent rankings list The Seminole Golf Club as #12 in "America's 100 Greatest Courses."[10]

PAGES 106-107
The swimming pool and tennis court as seen from the north wing, circa 1930.

PAGES 108-109
Wyeth's classical Spanish clubhouse for Seminole was built along the Atlantic Ocean, a centerpiece for Donald Ross's world-famous golf course.

CHAPTER SEVEN

THE SPANISH COURTYARD HOUSE

All the rooms in the Spanish House open on to the patio.[1]

—R. W. Sexton, *Spanish Influence on American Architecture and Decoration*, 1927

hen Marion Sims Wyeth moved to Palm Beach in 1919, he was enveloped in Addison Mizner's embrace of the Mediterranean Revival style and observed: "We all followed [Mizner's] lead. His dream was to have a city of red tile roofs. And we were all influenced by that dream."[2] One form of that style which Wyeth perfected was the Spanish courtyard house. For a house that was built on an interior lot and had neither ocean nor lakefront exposure, the enclosed courtyard plan turned the house inward away from the street allowing owners to take advantage of the south Florida winter weather while maintaining the privacy of their homes. In a time before air-conditioning, this was a desirable dividend. The courtyards in these houses were surrounded by covered cloisters offering shade and fresh air, protected from the sunshine. The outdoor space offered sun during the day, with ever changing light, and the night sky to light up evening entertaining. These houses also continued the centuries old tradition of the hidden patio and garden inherited from the Moorish influence on Spanish architecture. They often incorporated a fountain in the middle of the space.

Wyeth's interpretations of this Spanish Courtyard style combined many of the details that were so important for the successful implementation of the Palm Beach fantasy. Addison Mizner romanticized the idea that houses should appear as if they belonged to a family for generations even though that would have been impossible at the inception of the young Palm Beach resort. Applied ornamentation placed on rusticated stucco walls was a device to achieve an effect of age and ancestry. Wrought iron grills and railings, Spanish tiles, glazed pottery and stone shields with imagined heraldry were all essential to evoke an air of pedigree. Since these decorative resources were not readily available in south Florida in the 1920s, Mizner created his own business to manufacture these fabricated antiques. Mizner

110

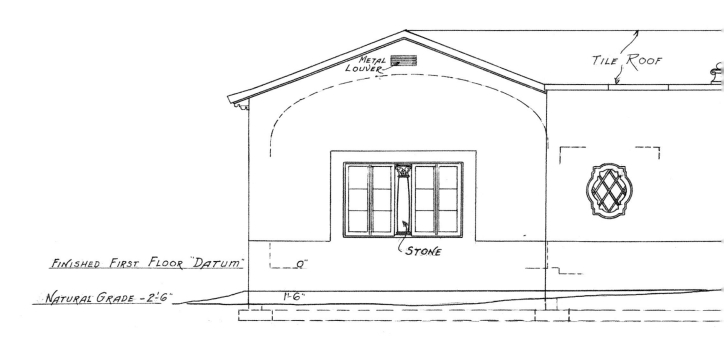

Industries was born of both demand and need and located conveniently just across Lake Worth in West Palm Beach. If you did not have authentic Cuban tiles for your roof, an architect specified a "Modern Cuban Roof" and bought the tile from Mizner. If he did not have the ancient stone columns he needed to support the cloister or porch, a cast stone column, manufactured with coquina, limestone and cement from Mizner Industries would fit the bill. A material called "woodite," made of wood shavings and plaster of Paris cast in a pre-made mold, was used for wall paneling and ceilings. Staged authenticity was the fashion of the day.

THE RECTORY

Now an integral part of the campus of the Episcopal Church of Bethesda-by-the-Sea in Palm Beach, Florida, the Rectory began life as a private single-family house. It was designed in December 1924 by Marion Sims Wyeth for Mr. and Mrs. Edward E. Jenkins, who arrived in south Florida from East Hampton, New York. Jenkins was a developer and quickly sold his new house to Malcolm Meacham, his recently married business partner in the Olympia Improvement Company.

Called Casa Bougainville when it was owned by the Meachams, the house is a perfect example of the Spanish courtyard house. The one-story structure faces south on Barton Avenue. It is asymmetrical in elevation and when approached all eyes turn to the elaborate front entrance in the center of the facade. A segmented arch springs from cast-stone pilasters topped with classical capitals on either side of the opening. Above the door a stone shield announces the imagined pedigree of the occupants. A dripstone embraces the door from above surrounding the design of the arch and the shield. Dripstones originated during the Romanesque period in Europe as a way of keeping rainwater away from an opening. Later they became a decorative element and were almost universal in Gothic architecture in parts of Germany, France and Spain. Above this design a pediment and cartouche top the entrance.

When the pecky cypress front doors of the house are closed, the resident has complete privacy. When they are opened, the visitor looks in to see a fountain

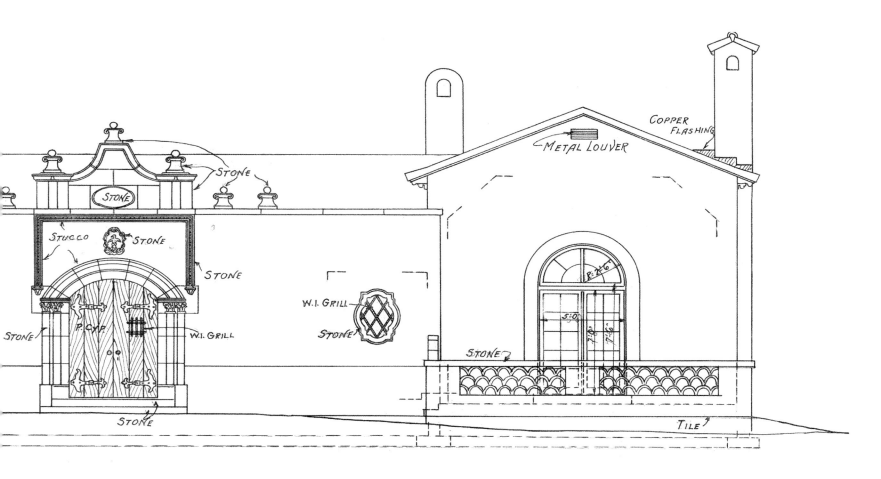

The hidden courtyard, so familiar in Spanish-Moorish architecture, is glimpsed through an elaborate arched entrance.

FOLLOWING PAGES
When the door is closed at the Rectory, the interior space becomes totally private, allowing residents to enjoy Florida's sub-tropical climate.

113

The locations of the living room
and dining room were reversed
in 1929 when the house was
purchased by the Episcopal
Church of Bethesda-by-the-Sea.
Here the dining room is in its
original space.

116

HOUSE FOR FEE JENKINS
PALM BEACH - FLA.

88 | 1000

centered in an almost symmetrical courtyard surrounded by a cloister. In the floor-plan, all the public and private rooms originally opened to the patio just as Sexton described in 1927. Bedrooms were on the west and the living room was on the east with a cathedral coffered ceiling of stenciled décor and a courtyard terrace though the French doors to the south. There was a two-story garage in the rear of the house.

Tragedy struck the house in 1929. Even before the stock market crash in October of that year, Meachum who was overextended in his real estate developments on Singer Island and Key West, Florida, took his own life. The *Palm Beach Post* reported on March 14, 1929, that "Malcolm Meacham Dies in Eleven-Story Plunge; Was Prominent Realtor."[3] His family claimed it was an accident.

The house was sold to the church in April of 1929 for $55,000 to be used as the rectory, or home of the priest.[4] Wyeth, who was a member of the congregation, connected the two-story garage at the rear of the property to the main house in 1935 for much needed space. Even with this addition, the main Spanish courtyard house remained intact. It was landmarked by the Town of Palm Beach in 1990.

The stenciled ceiling of the living room had this snake motif for décor. The design was later thought to be inappropriate for the church and was removed.

117

ABOVE AND FACING PAGE
The living room of the house was converted
to the dining room for the church in 1929.
The fireplace remained intact, but the
snake stenciling on the ceiling was removed.

FOLLOWING PAGES
The cloister and low Moorish
fountain at the Rectory.

An outside gallery on the second floor offers a view of the courtyard below.

FACING PAGE
Many of the elements of the Spanish courtyard house can be seen in Tre Fontaine. The outside staircase, covered cloister and low central fountain all combine to create a beautiful open space.

TRE FONTAINE

Marion Sims Wyeth got the inspiration for his personal Spanish courtyard residence during a trip to Spain. It was 1923, and he had just successfully finished the Golf View Road Development project. He traveled abroad for both relaxation and to find new ideas for his architectural practice. Although he had spent a lot of time in Italy as a student, he had never been to Spain to absorb its confluence of Iberian, Roman and Moorish culture. He visited Madrid and Barcelona but also took side trips to Ronda and Granada to see the Alhambra. He landed on the island of Majorca after an overnight boat ride from the mainland. The experience added to his architectural palette. Wyeth described his new residence Tre Fontaine or "Three Fountains" which was completed in 1924 in an oral history from 1980:

> In 1923, Eleanor and I went to Spain. We had a very nice time, and when I came back, I built a Spanish home for myself on Middle Road. We went and visited the island of Majorca and fell in love with some of the architectural things they had there. The house was based on that type of thing where you come into a patio with a cloister all around it, and you'd go out of doors to go upstairs—under cover, but out of doors. There was no inside staircase. The corridor off of the bedrooms upstairs was a porch facing west, and the four bedrooms faced east.[5]

True to its name, Wyeth's home had three low fountains centered on the front door and placed on an east–west access through the heart of the house. From the street, the west facade is simple and plain with an asymmetrical articulation. The front entrance is the main focus. Reached by climbing a few low steps with a curved wrought iron railing, the door is surrounded by irregular quoins and topped with a rounded arch. Applied ornamentation in the form of a stone shield is balanced above the door as part of a beautifully expressed dripstone.

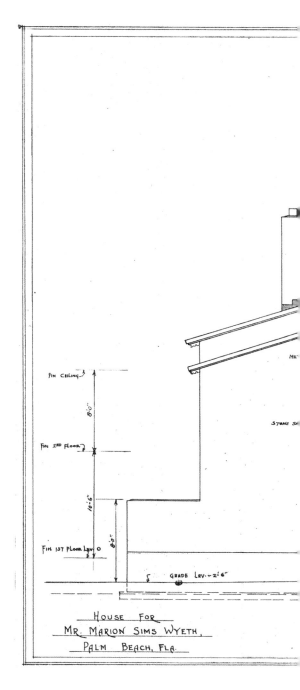

House for
Mr. Marion Sims Wyeth,
Palm Beach, Fla.

TOP LEFT
The front entry with hood
molding on the west facade.

LEFT
David McCulloch, Marion Sims
Wyeth and Addison Mizner in
the courtyard at Tre Fontaine.

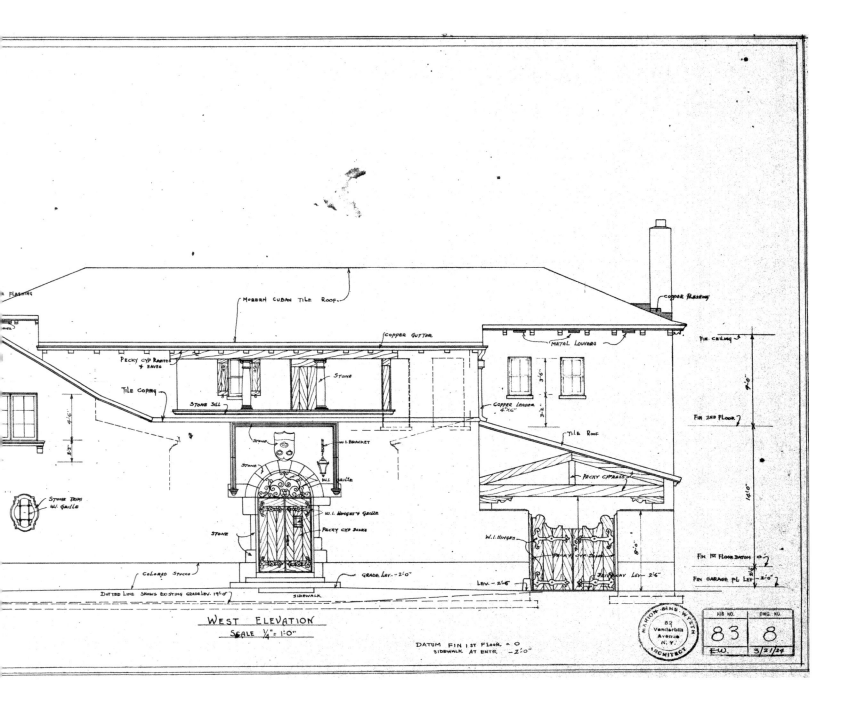

WEST ELEVATION
SCALE ¼" = 1'-0"

DATUM FIN 1ST FLOOR = 0
SIDEWALK AT ENTR. -2'-0"

The interior of Wyeth's house surprises you the moment you enter. The courtyard is a perfect square, an interior garden that must be navigated to access the rest of the rooms. The columns that support the arched cloister have foliated capitals in contrast to the more simplified Ionic capitals on the second-floor gallery that is visible above. The loggia is straight ahead with the living room and dining room on either side. Bedrooms are on the second floor, reached by an outside staircase accessed through the cloister. One surprise is that the ceilings of the public rooms are all different and it has been suggested that Wyeth did this to show examples of this work to prospective clients. The living room has a stenciled, coffered ceiling. The dining room has a simpler cross-beamed ceiling and the loggia's ceiling is supported by groin vaults and corbels giving the illusion of being vaulted.

Wyeth used his personal residence for entertaining and an occasional client stayed the night. During the 1930s, he leased the house to prospective clients for a month or two of high season and moved the family to a rental property. Tre Fontaine was after all the perfect Spanish Courtyard house and a great example of his work. The house was landmarked by the Town of Palm Beach in 1990.

The original loggia
had the second of
the three fountains
in its center.

The living room, dining room and
loggia (on the following pages) each
have a different ceiling style. It has
been suggested that Wyeth's aim was
to show clients examples of his work.

128

CHAPTER EIGHT

A RETURN TO THE CLASSICS

Southern Colonial Architecture makes a Palm Beach Appearance.[1]

—The *Palm Beach Post*, December 2, 1934

hen the United States fell into the Great Depression in 1929, Palm Beach had already experienced a slowdown in the real estate frenzy of the 1920s. The collapse of Florida banks in 1926 along with devastating back-to-back hurricanes in 1926 and 1928 brought most of the building speculation in south Florida to a halt. Addison Mizner's Mizner Development Corporation filed for bankruptcy in September 1926 after overextending its business south into the development of the City of Boca Raton. Paris Singer ran into similar trouble with his real estate ventures on Singer Island and in 1927 he was arrested and charged with criminal fraud for deceptive advertising. Even the Everglades Club's future was in doubt for a time until a group of members purchased the club and its debt through the formation of the Everglades Protective Syndicate. Eventually, in 1936, the name of the residential street called Singer Place was changed to Middle Road as residents forgot Mr. Singer's accomplishments and sought to distance themselves from his scandals.[2]

Despite these downturns, construction never completely stopped in Palm Beach as it did in other communities. Instead, houses were reduced in size and styles were simplified, returning to tried and true classical architectural forms. The Spanish or Mediterranean style gave way to the Colonial Revival in all its forms from British Colonial to Neoclassical Revival, including houses with Regency and Georgian influences. The Monterey style, a hybrid of the others, came east from Northern California adding another variation to the trend. Dining rooms got smaller as the buffet replaced large dinner parties. Servants' areas were reduced, but every house now needed a garage. The era of over-the-top palaces and impressive stage sets for a handful of grandes dames was over. As the *Palm Beach Post* reported, "The million-dollar Palm Beach palace is as obsolete as the Gibson girl."[3]

As times and architectural tastes changed Marion Sims Wyeth continued on without controversy or scandal. Wyeth's background and talent, grounded in the foundation of his classical architectural education, set the stage for his next decade of accomplishments.

A lacey wrought iron balcony
cantilevered over the front door is
centered on the east facade.

SOUTHWOOD

On December 28, 1934, Dr. and Mrs. John A. Vietor arrived in Palm Beach from New York on Vietwood, their private rail car. John Vietor was a world-renowned surgeon and his wife, Eleanor Woodward Vietor was the daughter of Orator F. Woodward who had founded the Genesee Pure Food Company in LeRoy, New York, and later developed the famous Jell-O gelatin dessert. The year 1934 would be the Vietors first New Year at their spacious lakefront estate on Via Del Lago. Called Southwood, the house was designed by Marion Sims Wyeth and built by H. R. Corwin, the contractor who had worked with Wyeth on the development of Golf View Road. Ruby Ross Wood, an interior designer of some renown, traveled south from New York to complete the decoration.

It was said that Eleanor Vietor wanted a house based on eighteenth-century Georgian architecture from Charleston, South Carolina. Wyeth fulfilled this wish with a house that combines Southern Colonial and Monterey style features in an overall effect that became known as Tropical Colonial. The cost of the project was reported to be $190,000.[4]

When driving into the motor court the first thing you notice is the large banyan tree centered in the circular drive. Although the tree looks like it has been there for generations, in reality it was part of the original 1934 landscape design completed by the Boynton Landscape company. Wyeth called for this plant material and also the use of palmetto palms around the property rather than Palm Beach's usual

coconut palms in an effort to evoke South Carolina at the moment of your arrival. A cantilevered balcony with lacey cast iron railings and arches extends across the central block of the east facade, conjuring romanticized places in the American South. The door itself features an elliptical fanlight over the entrance and sidelights are framed by engaged Ionic columns. The name Southwood is incised for perpetuity over the door. Windows are a classical sash style with shutters.

Marion Sims Wyeth's U-shaped plan for Southwood is one he used throughout his career and executed in varying styles for various locations. In this case he also included a perpendicular service wing along the south side of the house for kitchen, staff and garage. The patio and primary outdoor space are to the west, taking advantage of a wonderful view of Lake Worth. An open loggia is on the north leading to a later party room addition with a swimming pool centered on the west facade. At the south side of the pool, two small turreted dressing rooms designed to resemble Charleston tea houses serve as cabana baths. The *Palm Beach Post* was effusive in its description and praise for the house: "Smooth white walls and gray blinds ... intricate tracery of cast iron balcony rails ... fanlights above the doorways ... classic archways and hand carved chair rail trim ... simplicity of line ... all blended into a background, harmoniously combined with modern luxury and convenience."[5] The house was praised when it was built and landmarked by the Town of Palm Beach in 1990.

135

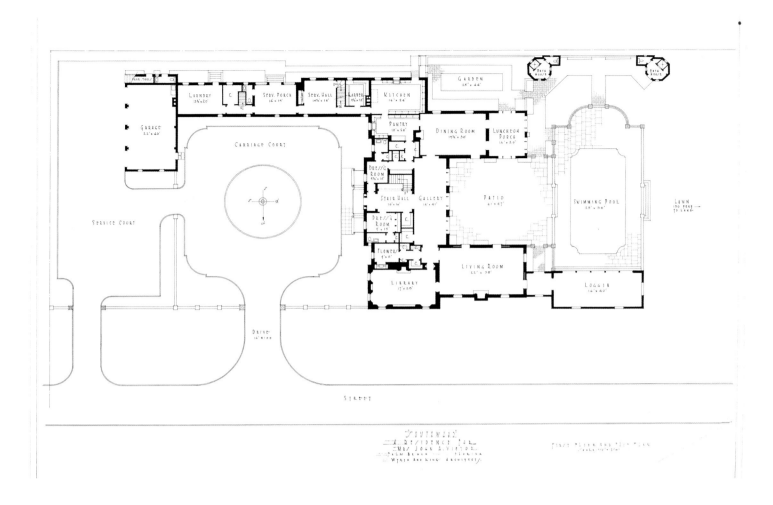

An etched glass mirror in the bar addition to the house was completed in 1940.

FACING PAGE
The gallery connects the north and south wings of the house and opens to a view of Lake Worth on the west. The elliptical fanlights over the patio doors echo the front entrance.

ABOVE AND FACING PAGE
Called the "Luncheon Patio" on
Wyeth's floorplan, this informal
dining area is surrounded with
garden views. On the left is the
room as it was designed by New
York decorator Ruby Ross Wood
and, on the right, after renovation.

The south side of the house
is surrounded by gardens and
quiet areas.

RIGHT
Looking north to the pool and
outdoor loggia.

FOLLOWING PAGES
An elegant pool area with a central
fountain and stone balusters looks
over the lake shore.

Joseph M. Cudahy

The gable-roofed entrance portico
has Doric columns and is enclosed
with louvered panels that give the
house a British West Indian feel.

CUDAHY HOUSE

Born in Chicago, Illinois, Joseph M. Cudahy was the heir to the Armour-Cudahy Meat Packing fortune and his wife Jean was the Morton Salt heiress. The Cudahy's built their first Palm Beach house in 1922, using Addison Mizner for their architect. By 1937, their taste had changed, along with that of the community and they hired Marion Sims Wyeth to build them something different on the newly renamed Middle Road. If Southwood's owners patterned their southern-style Palm Beach home on the precedent of structures in Charleston, South Carolina, Joseph and Jean Cudahy favored a more simplified British Colonial design patterned on the Caribbean.

Working with a corner lot, Wyeth started his plan for Cudahy House with an L-shaped floorplan that fronted on Middle Road and extended east along the north side of the lot toward the ocean. Jack S. Willson was the contractor and the cost were reported to be $90,000.[6]

The transom topped front door of Cudahy House is centered on the west facade and entered through a one-story porch with a gable roof that has a broken pediment reflecting a Georgian inspiration. The porch is light and airy, held up by slender Doric columns. Simple colonial pickets enclose the bottom of the porch and the shuttered infill on the sides adds to an island feel. Two symmetrical wings come off the central entry block and terminate with matching bay windows. A third bay window appears on the east facade. Other colonial details include a raised belt course between floors, sash windows with shutters, and quoining at the corners of the structure.

In contrast to the small entry porch, the main roof on the house is an intersection of hip roofed areas. The eaves are shallow and decorated with dentils in the central block. In the rear of the house gabled dormers and cupolas break up the expanse of the roof and add interest. Today many of these dormers have Bahama shutters, again reflecting an island ambiance. Over the years, a pool and outdoor loggias have been added. What was once an open porch on the south side of the house has been enclosed for a study. Even with these changes, the integrity of Wyeth's design is intact. Cudahy House was landmarked by the Town of Palm Beach in 1990 and won the Preservation Foundation of Palm Beach's Ballinger Award in 2018.

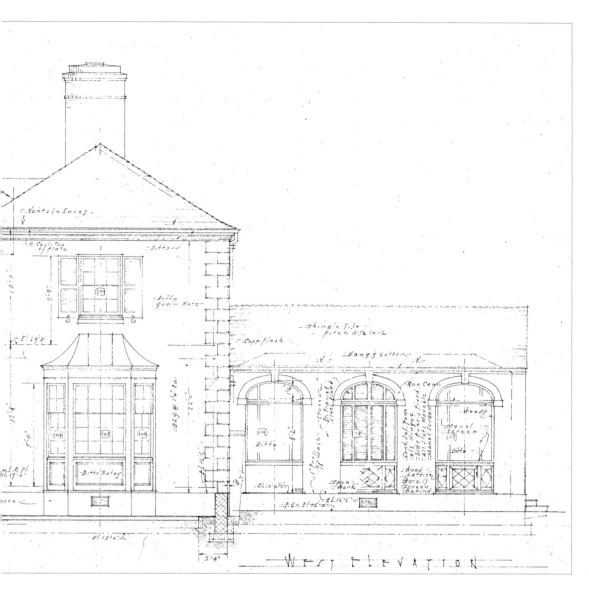

The house has a multi-level roofline with shutters, dormers and a cupola on the ridge line.

149

The Neoclassical temple front portico with four Ionic columns graces South Ocean Boulevard.

SHAUGHNESSY HOUSE

On July 3, 1938, the *Palm Beach Post* reported that a "Large Home will be Constructed for Mrs. Francis A. Shaughnessy." At an estimated cost of $117,000, the job was projected to be the largest building project of the Palm Beach summer. The Neoclassical Greek Revival–style home was designed by Marion Sims Wyeth and the contractor was C. J. Trevail. Polly Jessup was the interior decorator.[7]

Mrs. Jesse Hood Bassett Shaughnessy was the widow of two wealthy and influential men. Her first husband was Harry Bassett, who was a General Motors auto magnet; and her second husband was Francis A. Shaughnessy, who had been the president and director of the First National Bank in Palm Beach from its inception

The pool with an elegant lanai.

in December 1927 until his death in 1936. Mrs. Shaughnessy herself became an important philanthropist in the West Palm Beach area in 1938 when she donated a fully equipped twelve room addition to Good Samaritan Hospital in memory of Mr. Shaughnessy, who had served as treasurer to the hospital board.[8]

For Shaughnessy House, Marion Sims Wyeth repurposed the two-story U-shaped plan he used so often and took advantage of the layout of the land and setting as he often did. Built on an oceanfront lot where South Ocean Boulevard makes a sharp turn to the west onto Barton Avenue, the orientation of this house is unique. What is interesting is that the front entrance avoids the ocean view to the east and instead looms over the front drive, a public statement of style and grandeur. The distinctive Neoclassical Greek temple-front portico is centered in the middle of the symmetrical south facade. Four two-story columns topped with

The two-story entry hall is beautified by an elegant stair rail and checkerboard floor.

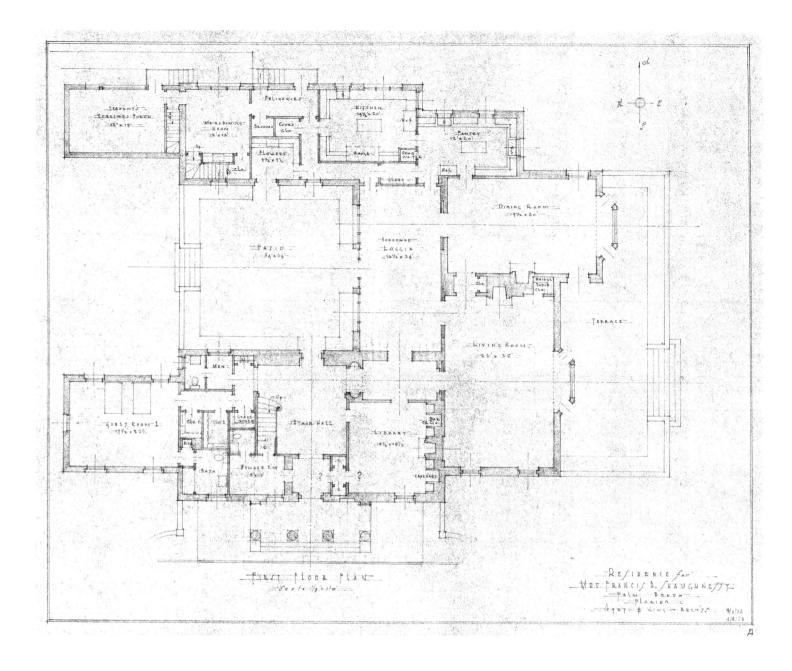

Ionic capitals rise to meet the pediment above. Sash windows have shutters and the truncated hip roof on the central block gives height to the design. At your point of entry, the ocean is of little consequence.

Once inside the two-story stair hall with the original checkerboard tile pattern on the floor, the visitor views a courtyard and patio through the opening ahead. This outdoor space between the two wings of the plan faces west protecting the family and their guests from sometimes strong ocean breezes. Then, as if guided to another world the architect turns you to the right for a spectacular glimpse of the Atlantic Ocean, seen beyond the twenty-two-foot-by-thirty-five-foot living room. Wyeth has placed the living room and dining room with direct unobstructed ocean views, doing what he enjoyed in many projects, bringing the outside in. Since its construction, Shaughnessy House has undergone a number of additions and renovations but retains its integrity. The house was landmarked by the Town of Palm Beach in 1993 and won the Preservation Foundation's Ballinger award in 1999.

CHAPTER NINE

PRESERVING THE FABRIC OF PALM BEACH

I give thanks to all who have worked so hard to keep Palm Beach beautiful.... Don't Falter. Keep on fighting.[1]

—Barbara D. Hoffstot

n historic preservation circles, Barbara D. Hoffstot (1919–1994) was a force to be reckoned with. She believed passionately in saving the historic character of both Palm Beach, Florida, and Pittsburgh, Pennsylvania, the communities she lived in and loved. She served on historic preservation boards in both locations and was appointed a trustee to the National Trust for Historic Preservation. During the 1950s, '60s and '70s, Palm Beach saw the demolition of a number of grand old estates, due to high property taxes and developers hungry to subdivide large parcels for more profitable land use. In 1974, Barbara's book *Landmark Architecture in Palm Beach* called attention to these demolitions and the need for a landmark's preservation ordinance to protect what was left. Ever the activist, Barbara not only called attention to the problem but worked on the solution, drafting Palm Beach's original landmark ordinance with the help of her husband, attorney Henry Phipps Hoffstot, Jr. In 1979 the Palm Beach Preservation Ordinance was passed, and since that time hundreds of historic properties have been designated and saved. As of 2021, Barbara's groundbreaking book has also endured and, with the support of the Preservation Foundation of Palm Beach, is now in its fourth edition.

If it was not for the efforts of pioneer preservationists like Barbara Hoffstot and the creative thinking and commitment of owners, restoration architects, the Preservation Foundation of Palm Beach, and the Landmarks Preservation Commission, some of Marion Sims Wyeth's most important buildings would have been lost. All these renovations were a challenge. All the results were a success.

The original front door of Bienestar. Although no longer operative, its beauty enriches the west facade.

A comparison of a 1924
photograph of the exterior with
a contemporary image shows the
quality of the adaptive reuse.

BIENESTAR

Designed in 1924 for Frederick S. Wheeler, the Chairman of the American
Can Company, Bienestar, whose name means "Wellbeing," was one of Marion Sims
Wyeth's early Mediterranean Revival–style designs. Built around a courtyard, the
elaborately molded front door and carved stone balcony on the west facade of the
house have a definite Venetian Gothic feel. A hanging wooden balcony around the
interior patio, along with wrought iron and cast stone details throughout the house,
add to the décor.

Located on Grace Trail on a generous acre of land, the lot size and underlying
zoning almost led to the destruction of the estate when the property changed hands
in 1985. This house had not been landmarked in 1979 after the passage of the

Landmarks Preservation Ordinance, and the land was zoned for six units. Demolition was a definite possibility. Luckily for Wyeth's legacy, the property was bought by a developer who was also a committed preservationist. Robert T. Eigelberger sat on the Landmarks Commission and had already completed the restoration and conversion of a nearby Addison Mizner villa into condominiums. With permission of the Palm Beach Town Council he used the same strategy for Bienestar. "One advantage of dividing a large house like Bienestar," Eigelberger stated at the time, "is that each owner will have a totally individual unit. Not one will be like the other."[2] When the project was finished, Eigelberger voluntarily designated Bienestar assuring its protection for future generations. The project was so successful that in 1988, Bienestar, coupled with Eigelberger's earlier project Warden House received the Preservation Foundation's first Ballinger Award.

FOLLOWING PAGES
Historic photographs of the interior illustrate the luxurious lifestyle of the 1920s.

163

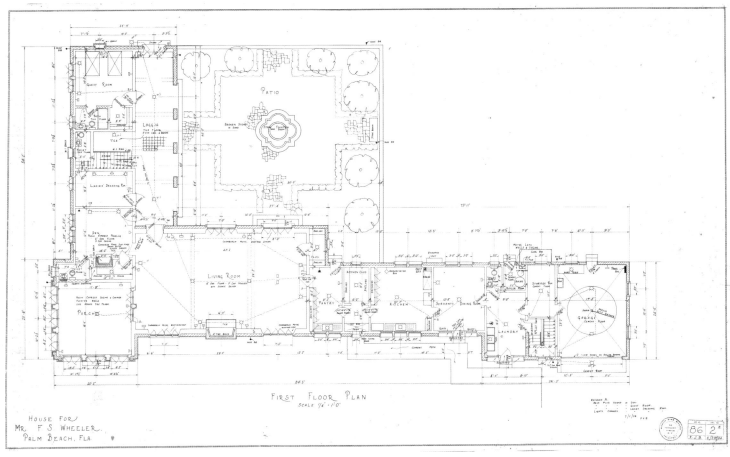

A cast stone cantilevered balcony adds romance to the Mediterranean Revival facade.

FACING PAGE
Bienestar's central courtyard is embellished with a three-tiered fountain and lush garden.

Raising Villa Tramento helped protect the house from high water and rising tides on Lake Worth.

The east facade of Villa Tramento shows Venetian design details, like the Lion of Venice and Gothic ogee arches, reimagined by Wyeth for Palm Beach.

VILLA TRAMENTO

In 1925, Marion Sims Wyeth designed a two-story Venetian Gothic–style house that boasted cast stone reliefs of the famous Lion of Venice and its own gondola slip for Frederick Glidden, whose father Francis had founded the Glidden Paint and Varnish Company. Originally from Cleveland, Ohio, the Gliddens were long-time visitors to Palm Beach, active in the Everglades Club and founders of the Animal Rescue League.

Although situated in a subdivision called Vita Serena, which means "Peaceful Life," the reality of living in a Venetian-style villa on the banks of Lake Worth was anything but peaceful. During extreme high tides, tropical storms and hurricanes, anecdotal reports indicate that the first floor flooded when the lake rose, while owners and staff struggled to move valuables to the second floor. Landmarked in 1989, the house was due for a complete renovation in 2002, when owners decided to address the low elevation and problems of *Aqua Alta* or "High Water," as the Venetians would have called it. Lifting a house is never easy but this was especially difficult because the structure had been built so close to the water's edge. The

TILE ROOF

EAST ELEVATION
SCALE ¼" = 1'-0"

HOUSE FOR
FRED A. GLIDDEN ESQ.
PALM BEACH FLA.

PREVIOUS PAGES
The western facade as seen
from Lake Worth.

elevation of the surrounding street scape had to be taken into account and ultimately the small road in front of the house also had to be raised so the house would not loom over the street. With the approval of the Landmarks Preservation Commission, a second-story addition was added, and the house was raised three feet. The project was a success and solved the problem of rising water. A subsequent owner completed further renovations, redoing the pool area, which was not original to the house, and adding an outside loggia for beautiful evenings overlooking Lake Worth and the skyline of nearby West Palm Beach. A landmark threatened by environmental problems had been saved.

172

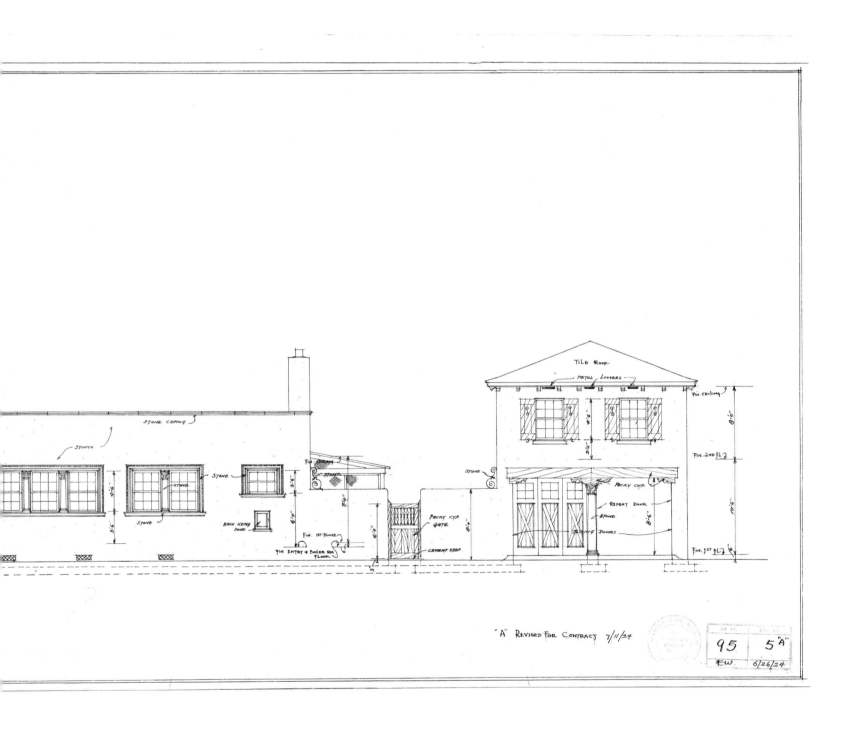

"A" Revised For Contract 7/11/24

95	5 "A"
E.W.	6/26/24

173

The entry hall and staircase.

RIGHT
The living room retains
the stenciled ceilings.

ABOVE AND FACING PAGE
The den exudes a quiet atmosphere
while the new outdoor loggia provides
a covered patio to enjoy views of Lake
Worth.

A new lakefront pool area was added to the south of the house while an outside gate suggests the doorways of Venice with twisted columns and a Venetian Gothic ogee top.

The original entrance was approached around a circular motor court that stopped in front of the three-story Moorish-style tower.

FACING PAGE
The historic entrance now faces the pool in the subdivided property.

CIELITO LINDO

The forty-five-thousand-square-foot, one-hundred-and-twenty-five-room winter home of James P. and Jesse Woolworth Donahue was the largest single-family home Marion Sims Wyeth designed in Palm Beach. Called Cielito Lindo or "A Little Piece of Heaven," the house had cost over $2,000,000 and was built in 1927 on a sixteen-acre parcel of land that extended from the Atlantic Ocean to Lake Worth with three hundred feet of ocean frontage and a beachfront lot across A1A. Jesse Donahue was the youngest daughter of F. W. Woolworth, the founder of the Woolworth Five-and-Ten-Cent Stores who, when he died in 1919, was one of the wealthiest men in America. A newspaper article at the time of construction described the house: "Like most Palm Beach homes built by Mr. Wyeth, the architecture is decidedly Spanish in feeling and influence and the dominant feature will be the patio facing west and overlooking the lake with a glass terrace above it."[3] It also had many Moorish Revival details, especially in the tower and the entryway. The grounds were elaborate as well and included houses for the gardener and chauffeur, a tennis court, boat house, orange groves and a tea pavilion. When everything was finished, the *New York Evening Post* reported that "the mansion takes its place among the four or five of Palm Beach's most notable homes."[4]

Although the swimming pool on the postcard was in the west yard, it was well south of the central patio. The scene in the postcard was foreshortened to place both the house and pool in a single view.

FACING PAGE
Sketch of the Moorish tower at Cielito Lindo

The living room of Cielito Lindo was removed when the property was subdivided into five villas. Kings Road now runs through this space.

FACING PAGE
The mansion's original entry hall.

After World War II, Jesse Donahue, who was then a widow, decided to simplify and downsize her Palm Beach winters. She took an apartment at the Everglades Club and in 1946 sold Cielito Lindo to developers for $101,000. She did reserve the beach front lot and one section in the property for a guest house. Most believed the house would be demolished like other large properties from the 1920s, but architect Byron Simonson of the firm Simonson and Holley, devised a plan to subdivide the land into nineteen lots and partition the large mansion into five smaller villas. A new road would be built and Kings Road, as it was called, ran through the large sixty-foot living room. *Palm Beach Life* reported that "dining halls became living rooms in the partitioning, servant's quarters were converted into bedrooms and even an incinerator flu became a fireplace…. Now stands on the site of the great Spanish-Moorish castle five smaller ones. All Cielito Lindo thus divided into five parts produced charming and intimate smaller villas, picturesquely dotting a broad expanse stretching from the ocean to lake along Kings Road in the new Ocean Boulevards Estates."[5]

The size and scale of Wyeth original masterpiece is gone but you can catch glimpses of the past grandeur when you look at the five houses carved out of the original. Two of the five at 122 and 123 Kings Road were landmarked in 2016, assuring that you can always find "A Little Piece of Heaven" in Palm Beach.

The loggia.

Carved on the garden wall of the estate is the name Cielito Lindo and the Latin phrase from Horace's Ode, 4:12 *"Dulce est desipere in loco"* which translates as "good to play the fool at times."

CHAPTER TEN

SHANGRI LA

I feel very sorry that this work has terminated as it has been one of the most interesting and thrilling jobs ever to be handled by this office.[1]

—Marion Sims Wyeth, December 1, 1939

W hen Doris Duke (1912–1993) quietly married James H. R. Cromwell on February 13, 1935, the headline the next day read "World's Richest Girl Married in New York."[2] No one could have imagined that a honeymoon that took the couple on a ten-month tour of the Middle East, India, Asia, and terminated in the United States Territory of Hawaii, would spark in the bride a lifelong passion for Islamic art and architecture. Marion Sims Wyeth could not have imagined that within a little more than a year he would receive one of the most important commissions of his career.

Doris Duke was the only child of James Buchanan Duke and his second wife Nanaline Holt Inman. "Buck" Duke made his fortune with the American Tobacco and Duke Energy Companies. When he died in 1925, Doris was twelve years old and inherited approximately eighty million dollars that was set up in trust to be distributed at milestone birthdays. On her twenty-first birthday she received ten million dollars with more to follow.

Duke's groom, the younger son of high-profile Palm Beach hostess Eva Cromwell Stotesbury was known as Jimmy. He was sixteen years older than the bride and correspondence shows that he had been pursuing the wealthy young girl for a number of years. Her reluctance to marry him, despite his charm and good looks, may have been based on apprehension about his past.[3] Jimmy Cromwell had married Delphine Dodge, the automobile heiress in 1920 and during their marriage entered into one disastrous business deal after another, primarily using Delphine's money. Cromwell was a shareholder in Addison Mizner's failed Boca Raton project. He invested in the Peerless Motor Company, which had several reversals, and finally became a partner in an advertising firm which "collapsed in scandal." His mother Eva Stotesbury and Delphine's mother Anna Dodge made good on approximately three million dollars of losses. Jimmy and Delphine had one daughter, but the marriage ended in divorce in 1928.[4]

Wyeth added cove lighting to the carved wooden ceiling fabricated in Morocco. On the far side of the room the large glass windows descend into the foundation to merge indoor and outdoor space.

FOLLOWING PAGES
Southeastern Oahu's rocky coastline showing Shangri La and the original boat basin that now provides public access to the Pacific Ocean.

In 1935, Jimmy's life began anew. The first stop in Doris and Jimmy's honeymoon was Monte Carlo, followed by Egypt, Jordan, and then on to India where, in Agra, Doris fell in love with the Taj Mahal. She was particularly enchanted by the marble tile with floral designs inlaid with semiprecious stones. Jimmy wrote home to his mother about plans to alter his Palm Beach villa, Malmaison, which was part of El Mirasol, the Stotesbury estate:

> Due to the India environment and cooking, plumbing was possibly the utmost thing in her mind, and the lovely bedroom she proposes to build for herself at Malmaison. She got her cue from the Taj Mahal and wanted her bedroom done in tiles like those in the Taj Mahal. She went to the factory in Agra, where they still do such work, and got all the advice. When we got back to Delhi we got hold of the best British architect—a Mr. Blomfield—and had him draw up some tentative plans and estimates[5]

Jimmy ended the letter to his mother with a request. "We would like to have your opinion about this as well as that of whichever architect you choose to do the work."[6] By May 1, Mrs. Stotesbury had picked Maurice Fatio of the Palm Beach firm Treanor and Fatio, and seemingly took charge.

Eleanor Fatio, the architect's wife, wrote about the situation on July 9, 1935, in a letter to Maurice's family in Switzerland:

> Jimmy [Cromwell] is the son of Mrs. Stotesbury and it has fallen to Maurice's lot, as her architect, to duplicate in Palm Beach the Taj Mahal, which caught Mrs. Cromwell's fancy when she was in India: marble is being shipped from India and Mrs. Stotesbury writes, telegraphs or telephones Maurice daily. The situation is made a little more difficult by the fact that Maurice is not even allowed to build from scratch but must transform Jimmy's former bachelor quarters into the gem of India … it really is the most preposterous assignment. We only hope that Mrs. Stotesbury will not order Maurice slain when the commission is executed.[7]

Eleonor Fatio, needn't have worried. In August, the newlyweds landed in Hawaii, and plans changed. The seeds of Shangri La had been planted.

Marion Sims Wyeth (left) and H. Drewry Baker (right) discuss plans with unknown woman on site in Hawaii.

Doris Duke at Shangri La, 1939.

Mr. and Mrs. James Cromwell arrived in Honolulu by ship and disembarked at Pearl Harbor. They registered at the Royal Hawaiian Hotel which opened in 1927 and was known as "The Pink Palace of the Pacific." Most notably for Doris, the couple met the Kahanamoku family. The five Hawaiian brothers were known as the "Waikiki Beach Boys" and encouraged Doris' infatuation with the islands by teaching her how to surf, sail an outrigger canoe and appreciate Hawaiian culture. They also persuaded her to extend her stay in Hawaii from two weeks to over three months. Jimmy flew home while Doris stayed to look for real estate with Sam Kahanamoku.

In February 1936, the newlyweds were in Palm Beach when a building permit was issued for the addition to Malmaison. Doris' mind, however, was in Hawaii. Jimmy wrote to Sam Kahanamoku from Palm Beach on March 10, 1936, approving the purchase of a property at Black Point for $100,000. He cautioned Sam to keep the transaction a "complete secret" by using his sister's name while negotiating.[8] The secret was out by April 4, 1936, when the *Honolulu Star-Bulletin* reported that: "The world's richest girl and her husband have fallen so deeply in love with Hawaii that they have decided to build a home…."[9] The 4.9-acre property included six hun-

A Spanish thirteenth-century marble fireplace in the living room was bought from the William Randolph Hearst collection in 1941. The coat of arms above the mantle was given to Doris's father, James Buchanan Duke, by the Turkish ambassador.

dred and fifty feet of Pacific Ocean shoreline between Diamond Head, a volcanic cone that rises over seven hundred feet above sea level, and the Kaalawai beach on the southeastern coast of the island of Oahu.

With the Hawaiian property secured, Doris Duke Cromwell abandoned the Palm Beach project. Shangri La was the only house she ever built from the ground up and she was not about to let her mother-in-law choose the architect. Instead, Doris turned to Marion Sims Wyeth. She knew Wyeth's work firsthand, as that spring she and Jimmy had hired him to complete alterations to her father's estate, Duke Farms, in Somerville, New Jersey. Wyeth had also just finished designing a house in Georgetown, South Carolina, for her half-brother Walker Inman. Newspaper accounts reported that Wyeth worked on plans with the couple throughout the summer of 1936.[10]

Then things hit a snag in Hawaii. The Cromwells asked to use territorial land at the water's edge to build a swimming pool and seawall on the beach next to their property. The plan was rejected by the Harbor Board. Editorials begged for a reversal so that the Cromwells would stay. Doris announced the sale of the Black Point property and requested that the marble and tiles that had been shipped to Hawaii from India be forwarded to Palm Beach. Palm Beach society crossed their fingers that the young couple would come to their senses and return to Florida. That was not to happen, and, in the end, the controversy was settled by giving the public access to the water in perpetuity. The building of Shangri La continued in Honolulu.[11]

Marion Sims Wyeth traveled to Hawaii to oversee the project twice in 1937, in February and again in August. He also appointed H. Drewry Baker, a young Princeton graduate and associate from his New York office, to stay in the islands and supervise construction. Wyeth's son, Buz, recalled that his father "took a three-day train trip across the country and then a ship out of San Francisco." He stayed six weeks to put the final touches on the plans and adjust the design according to the topography.[12] Wyeth later recounted that he took into account the possibility of earthquakes, "I used the San Francisco earthquake code, because you might easily have an earthquake there. These islands are all volcanic to begin with and by gosh they did have an earthquake after I built the house. I felt justified … spending an extra $50,000."[13]

194

The simple exterior of the entry courtyard adds an element of mystery to the approach.

The elaborate foyer was photographed in 1947 for *Town and Country Magazine.*

FACING PAGE
A separate guest suite named the Playhouse, 1947.

FOLLOWING PAGES
Cedar columns in the central courtyard were fabricated in Chicago based on photographs taken by the Cromwells in Isfahan, Iran, in 1938. Mirrors were applied to the them in 1941 adding shimmering light to the space. The central tile panel is from thirteenth-century Iran.

During the second trip, Wyeth stayed a month on the grounds in quarters that had been built and referred to as "architects' row."[14] The house was taking shape but the Cromwells startled Honolulu by naming their new home Hale Kapu which is Hawaiian for "forbidden house." The public was also surprised by descriptions that the house had only three bedrooms and one guest room. Mr. Wyeth was quoted as saying, "There'll be plenty of room."[15]

In actuality Doris Duke's new house was approximately fourteen-thousand square feet and was designed in a modernist style with connecting indoor and outdoor spaces that could adapt to her growing collection of Islamic art. She called the design "a Spanish-Moorish-Persian-Indian complex."[16] Thomas Mellon and Donald Albrecht writing in *Doris Duke's Shangri La: A House in Paradise* referred to this eclecticism as "inventive synthesis" and noted that the overarching umbrella for the idea of the house and collection was Duke's interest in the Islamic world as a whole rather than any geographical or historical moment. She used both original and commissioned pieces to create the desired effect.[17]

Although Shangri La is a reflection of its owner, many architectural concepts of the building show a connection to Wyeth's earlier work. The simplified entry block is reminiscent of his home Tre Fontaine, with a prominent door on a simple facade that does little to reveal the mystery beyond. Like Wyeth's Spanish patio houses of the 1920s, the courtyard is the heart of the house. The rooms used for entertaining radiate from this open space which features tile lined walls and doorways with mirrored columns that reflect the changing light. The entire area is surrounded by a covered walkway and centered on a low, star-shaped fountain embedded in the landscape.

A cascading water feature leads from the main house to the swimming pool and the Playhouse with iconic Diamond Head in the background.

The architectural elements of the living room include a coffered ceiling with an inscribed frieze that was commissioned in Morocco. Wyeth modernized this feature by adding cove lighting to draw your eye upward to the work of traditional craftsmanship that was so important to Doris Duke. He also used a device that was popular in Palm Beach at the time, a large window that lowers into the foundation to open the room to the landscape and erase the distinction between indoor and outdoor space. In this case, a twenty-one-foot pane-glass wall disappears so the living room becomes one with Diamond Head, the cascade pools to the west, and a distant building called the Playhouse on the far side of the swimming pool.

The Playhouse which contained the estate's only guest room was placed at the southwestern edge of the property. It is framed by Diamond Head and the sea, focusing our eyes on the environmental context of the estate. The building was inspired by the Chehel Sotoun, a Persian pavilion built in 1647 in Isfahan, Iran. The name literally means "Forty Columns," but in fact there are only twenty. The number is doubled in the viewer's eye because of the reflecting pool in front of the structure. Wyeth used a similar illusion for the Playhouse by placing the swimming pool in front of his building taking a traditional reference and making it residential and modern at the same time.[18]

Marion Sims Wyeth (third from left) and H. Drewry Baker (fifth from left) with Hawaiian coworkers during construction.

FOLLOWING PAGES
The dining room of Shangri La in 1947.

201

Construction of the dining
room, circa 1937.

FACING PAGE
A sea swept lanai off the dining
room decorated with mosaic tile
from Iran.

FOLLOWING PAGES
An early rendering of Shangri La
before plans were finalized.

Other important architectural elements include Doris' bedroom, called the Mogul suite, whose inspiration from the Taj Mahal and imported marble tiles started the whole project. A Mogul-inspired garden extends to the west of this wing while an outdoor staircase just to the south leads to the second floor. The dining room projects to the south of the house toward the Pacific Ocean and was originally contemporary in feel. It was redecorated during the 1960s but still contains the glass walls that lower into the foundation opening the interior to the environment.

Doris Duke and Jimmy Cromwell moved in on Christmas day 1938. They also changed the name of the house from Hale Kapu to Shangri La. Based on James Hilton's 1933 book *Lost Horizon* and the 1937 film, the house was no longer a "forbidden house," but was now "a place of beauty and harmony where people did not grow old."[19] At the time, a journalist wrote that Shangri La was "a perfectly cut gem with a flawless attention to detail, with a certain restraint that sparkles nonetheless."[20] When considering this against an overview of Marion Sims Wyeth's career, it would seem he had achieved his goal, architecture that was quiet, subdued and rational but in this case, also a canvas for his client's growing art collection. After protracted legal wranglings, Doris Duke's marriage to James Cromwell ended in 1943. Doris Duke passed away in 1993 and Shangri La now houses the Doris Duke Foundation for Islamic Art.

SOUTH EL

E   V   A   T   I   O   N

CHAPTER ELEVEN

NORTON GALLERY
AND SCHOOL OF ART

"For the Education and Enjoyment of the Public."

—Ralph Norton[1]

The Norton Gallery and School of Art in West Palm Beach, Florida, opened on February 8, 1941, to great local and national acclaim. Donated to the Palm Beach Art League by Ralph Hubbard Norton (1875–1953) the CEO of the Acme Steel Company and his wife, Elizabeth Calhoun Norton, the gift included a spectacular new building designed by Marion Sims Wyeth and an extensive private art collection. It also contained an endowment that was meant to help the museum in perpetuity and led to the reconfiguration of important road infrastructure in West Palm Beach, extending Flagler Drive south along Lake Worth to better access the gallery from the east. The *Palm Beach Post* reported that "the total investment is likely to approximate $1,000,000."[2] This generous gift established one of the first prominent art museums in south Florida, which today has been expanded and renamed the Norton Museum of Art.

Ralph Norton had been visiting Florida from Chicago since the late nineteenth century, and as he approached retirement he planned to build a winter home in Palm Beach. Instead, looking for a quieter lifestyle, he bought a property on Barcelona Road in the El Cid neighborhood of West Palm Beach. By the mid 1930s, the Mediterranean Revival–style house he had bought was outdated, and Norton hired Marion Sims Wyeth to remodel the house into a Monterey-style residence. Polly Jessup was asked to redo the interior design. The project lasted from 1935 to 1937 and helped shape a friendship and working relationship between the art collector and the architect.[4] Throughout this time, Ralph Norton's interest in collecting and purchasing art grew, and by all accounts he soon owned more paintings than walls to display them.

Originally, Norton thought that his private art collection might be given to the Society of the Four Arts in Palm Beach. Founded in 1934 by Mrs. Maud Howe Elliot, Mrs. Lorenzo E. Woodhouse and Mrs. Frederick Johnson, the society was

Entrance Hall, Norton Gallery
and School of Art, 1941.

Ralph Hubbard and Elizabeth
Calhoun Norton, circa 1941.

FACING PAGE
View across a painting gallery
with a bench by Jessup Inc. in
the center, 1941.

dedicated to the celebration of music, art, literature and drama. Both the Nortons
and Marion Sims Wyeth were among the inaugural members of the society's board
of Directors. During the 1937–38 season the Four Arts had an exhibit entitled "Contemporary American Painting from the Collection of Ralph H. and Elizabeth C.
Norton," showing fifty works from their private collection.[4] But complications with
the logistics of a donation arose over finances and the style of a proposed new
building, causing the hands-on collector and benefactor to reevaluate his decision
to leave his collection to the society.

Norton didn't have to go far from his residence to discover another possibility,
one that gave him complete control. Just to the north of his house, a piece of land
at Pioneer Park was empty. Comprising nearly half a city block, it was bounded
by Dixie Highway on the west and South Olive Avenue on the east, the two major
north/south arteries into West Palm Beach and perfect for his new gallery. Norton
added to the setting by purchasing the land to the east of the plot to establish a park
to showcase his museum with an Intracoastal view.

An anecdotal tale sometimes told about developing the concept for the new
building echos a common thread that surfaces throughout Marion Sims Wyeth's
career: the importance of friendship and personal relationships. One evening when
the Nortons were visiting their friend Polly Jessup's home, conversation turned to
the design of the future gallery. Jessup "called Wyeth who came over and began to
sketch a design in accordance with Ralph's idea that the new institution should have
a grand, Beaux Arts look like the Art Institute of Chicago."[5] Since the modern 1940s
version of the Beaux Arts style was Art Deco, the basics were established, decided
in a casual setting amongst friends. Wyeth took it from there. The development of
the original concept, however, was not a spur of the moment idea. "Norton later
recalled that he and Wyeth went to [visit] some of the large art galleries in the country to make sure we were making no mistakes in the design and plan of the gallery."[6]

210

INSCRIPTIONS
HERE ARE THE
SUBTLINGES

NORTON C

OLIVE STI

WYETH &

Pencil sketch of the Olive Street
elevation.

Marion Sims Wyeth's final design for the Norton Gallery and School of Art
had many innovations. The building was air-conditioned, which was rare in 1941,
to protect the artwork from Florida's humid climate. Natural light was brought into
the galleries through skylights. The plan included two separate sections that could
act independently, one for the museum and a second for the art school. A central
fifty-foot-by-one-hundred-foot courtyard in the art school wing was filled with native
plants to evoke the subtropical landscape of south Florida. And the courtyard itself,
although on a grander scale, harkened back to Wyeth's 1920s patio houses with the
goal of blending interior and exterior space.

The one-story museum section of the building faced South Olive Street with
a tripartite, symmetrical facade. The white bronze entry door with fluted pilasters
was centered in the design as two wings extend east toward the lake. The material
chosen for the exterior of the building was white stucco trimmed with Alabama
Rockwood Limestone. The roof had a lead-coated copper surface. This main elevation was sparse in ornamentation but with two empty niches in the wings it offered
an opportunity to make an artistic statement as well as show an architectural pres-
ence. Ralph Norton proposed two sculptors whose work might fill these spaces, but

212

ELEVATION

ARCHT'S

Marion Sims Wyeth took the lead and proposed a master of the mid-twentieth century. "Wyeth told Norton that the best artist for the commission would be Paul Manship, then the leading Art Deco sculptor in the United States."[7]

Paul Manship (1885–1966) was at the top of his career when Wyeth contacted him to supply sculptural pieces for the front of the Norton Gallery and School of Art. Manship, who designed mythological sculpture often in the classical style, was well known for his 1934 depiction of Prometheus at Rockefeller Center in New York City. Wyeth sent a sketch of the facade and pointed out the locations where the architect imagined sculpture. Wyeth suggested Manship could fill the niches with two pieces that had already been designed in the 1920s and which he had seen at the 1939 New York World's Fair.[8] He hoped the artist would create three new bas-reliefs for the panels above the niches and the front door. A price of $19,000 was negotiated which was over ten times the amount the other artists bid. It also brought the project $3,500 over budget. Wyeth wrote to Norton, "I feel that this is a very low price for what we are getting, and I sincerely hope you will agree with me…."[9] Ralph Norton agreed and the mythological figures of Diana and Actaeon took their places along South Olive Street. But not without controversy.

Close up of Diana, 2019.

FACING PAGE
Statue of Actaeon when it was installed in the south niche. Bas-relief by Paul Manship entitled Inspiration above, 1941.

PAGES 216-217
Wyeth's Olive Street facade for the Norton Gallery and School of Art with Paul Manship's sculptures returned to their narrative positions, 2018.

PAGES 218-219
Renovated central courtyard, 2018.

The story of Diana and Actaeon tells of the tale of the ancient Roman goddess of the hunt who is spied upon by young Actaeon while she bathes. Her revenge is to shoot him with her magical arrow and turn him into a stag whereupon he is devoured by his own dogs. Manship has chosen to depict this story at the moment of greatest tension. As she flees, Diana's bow is still raised. The arrow has found its target. Acteon holds his side as he runs in the opposite direction, but it is too late. Horns have started to sprout from his head and his dogs have caught a whiff of the stag he is morphing into. There is a strong narrative component to the work.

When Norton and Wyeth saw the sculptures installed, Norton objected to their perspective in the niches and had them reversed. In response to a 1985 newspaper article about the mysterious placement where Diana shots away from Acteon, William Royster Johnson, who had worked in the Wyeth & King office while the gallery was being designed and later became a partner in the firm Wyeth, King & Johnson, wrote a letter of explanation to the *Palm Beach Post*.

> I do not remember Marion Wyeth's reaction, but mine was that, aside from the "story telling" aspect, their relative positions made very little difference. Anyhow, after discussing the matter pro and con we phoned Paul Manship whose attitude was that the fable was of minor importance compared to aesthetic considerations, and by all means to reverse them if we thought best. Which, in effect, decided the matter.[10]

The sculptures were not restored to their narrative positions until 2002 and that is where they sit to this day.[11] Manship's bas-relief sculptures above the door and niches represent the attributes of good art and architecture, highlighting the eternal need for imagination, inspiration and interpretation in the creative process. And, eighty years after its opening, Marion Sims Wyeth's design for the Norton Gallery and Art School can still be described as a "beautiful building, modern and yet holding to eternal principles of the classic."[12]

214

BEAVTY IS TRVTH - TRVTH BEAVTY
THAT IS ALL YE KNOW ON EARTH
AND ALL YE NEED TO KNOW

CHAPTER TWELVE

THE FLORIDA GOVERNOR'S MANSION

It belongs to every citizen of Florida.

—Mary Call Collins, First Lady of Florida 1955–1961[1]

n 1950, Florida was booming. World War II had been over for five years and tens of thousands of servicemen and women who had trained in the sunshine state vowed to return, some as residents, some as visitors. According to the United States Census Bureau, Florida had become the twentieth largest state in the union with a total population of 2,771,305 people, a 46.1 percent increase from the previous decade. Miami, Jacksonville and Tampa were the largest cities. Palm Beach, the center of Marion Sims Wyeth's successful Florida architectural practice had a year-round population of 3,886.[2] But if World War II and a booming economy formed the basis for much of the state's expansion, the population would not have grown so quickly without two important developments in creature comforts: DDT, whose scientific name is Dichlorodiphenyltrichloroethane, was used to spray for mosquitoes, and air conditioning became affordable when window units came on the market in 1951.

With Florida experiencing prosperity and extraordinary growth, the state government also grew. The number of state representatives elected to go to Tallahassee increased and the role of the governor was expanded to focus on diplomatic tasks to promote statewide programs and initiatives. During this legislative expansion, a disagreement arose in Tallahassee over the fate of the old Governor's Mansion. Built in 1907 on a city block approximately one mile north of the state capital building, the southern style mansion at 700 North Adams Street was in such disrepair that, in 1949, Governor Fuller Warren had called it "The State Shack" and complained to the cabinet that he had to keep moving his bed to avoid falling plaster.[3] The condition of the house continued to deteriorate into the 1950s, and it became obvious that the old building had to either undergo a major renovation or be torn down and replaced with a new building. After a squabble over whether or not to restore

Governor Leroy Collins and his wife, Mary, moved into the Governor's Mansion with their children in 1957.

FOLLOWING PAGES
The Florida Governor's Mansion was inspired by Andrew Jackson's Greek Revival–style home, the Hermitage, in Nashville, Tennessee.

FIN. CEIL.

FIN 2ND FLOOR

FIN 1ST FL.

FIN. GRADE

APPROX GRADE

FIN. GROUND FL.

EAST ELEVATION
Scale 1/8"=1'-0"

WEST ELEVATION
Scale 1/8"=1'-0"

EXECUTIVE MANSION FOR THE STATE OF FLORIDA
TALLAHASSEE· FLORIDA

WYETH, KING & JOHNSON
ARCHITECTS
WYETH BUILDING, PALM BEACH, FLORIDA

Wyeth used the topography of the land so the building looked like a traditional two-story design on the east, while the three-story west facade contained staff entrances and offices.

EXECUTIVE MA
~ Tal
Wyeth, King & John

...SION for the STATE of FLORIDA
...hassee Florida ~
~Architects~ Palm Beach, Florida

SCHEL...

the old building or replace it, the issue was settled in 1953 when repair costs were estimated to top $135,000.[4] Legislators thought this amount was excessive for repair, and instead appropriated $250,000 for the construction of a new up-to-date residence for the state's top executive. They also determined that the new Governor's Mansion should be patterned on the Hermitage, President Andrew Jackson's home outside of Nashville, Tennessee. "It was fitting," they said, "that the mansion bear resemblance to General Jackson's home, for he was appointed the first American governor of Florida shortly after the territory was acquired from Spain in 1821."[5]

Although the construction of a new building was agreed upon, in Tallahassee the location was still contested. Some legislators and local real estate interests felt the Governor's Mansion should be relocated outside of town on a larger site with more parking, while preserving the original house in the city center as an historic landmark.

Statewide many people objected to modeling the house on the Hermitage. Newspapers suggested that the architecture "should be a type that is typical of this fast-growing sunshine state and not copied after some ancient architecture of another state."[6] Perceiving regional differences, Miami architects suggested that the mansion should be designed in a more contemporary style. "Tallahassee [they noted] is 'deep south' and has little resemblance to cosmopolitan Miami."[7]

In the end, thirteen other parcels of land were considered as possible building sites, but all were rejected. The mansion would be rebuilt in the old location. The use of the Hermitage as the inspiration for the new project, on the other hand, was confirmed and ratified. In 1955, Governor Leroy Collins announced that a selection committee headed by Robert H. Brown, the architect-engineer for the Board of Commissioners of State Institutions and composed of architects John L. Volk, Gustav Mass and Marion Sims Wyeth of Palm Beach, along with James Gamble Rogers of Winter Park and Earnest Stidolf of Tallahassee, was appointed to collectively make the decision on who would get the commission to design the new Florida Governor's Mansion. By the time deliberations were concluded, sixty-seven-year-old Marion Sims Wyeth of the firm Wyeth, King & Johnson had been selected.[8] The press was enthusiastic and almost uniformly called Wyeth "one of Florida's most noted architects."[9] Governor Collins was pleased because Wyeth "was also known to employ a cost-conscious spirit when designing all public projects."[10]

Wyeth began his creative thinking by traveling to Nashville, Tennessee, for a tour of Andrew Jackson's nineteenth-century plantation house, so he could absorb the feeling and scale of the original. Back in Tallahassee he also took into account the contour of the land where the building would be located, noting that there is a steep hill on the property that he wanted to use to his advantage. Further challenges arose when Governor Collins appointed a mansion advisory committee to collaborate on the design. This committee included six prominent Tallahassee citizens. More comments were solicited from state cabinet members and their wives. When asked by the press why the cabinet committee numbered fourteen, Collins replied, "That's the seven cabinet members and our wives. You might as well recognize the fact that they're going to be on this thing too."[11] So Marion Sims Wyeth began designing the Florida Governor's Mansion with the input of twenty well-intentioned lay people and by most accounts took it all in stride. He also cut his commission from the usual ten to fifteen percent to the rate of eight percent, stating that "it was because of the value to the firm of designing the 'monumental' structure."[12]

The main challenge involved in designing the Governor's Mansion, besides having to please prominent citizens, and politicians and their wives, was that the building had to serve a dual purpose. It had to be the personal home for the chief executive of Florida and his family, but it also had to have official rooms for receptions and state functions, office space for the governor and his staff, and guest rooms for visiting dignitaries and friends. Wyeth had to put all of these requirements into a Greek Revival-style shell that referenced a far-off historic building. The project was

Open Porch
(Doors in Rear Wall)

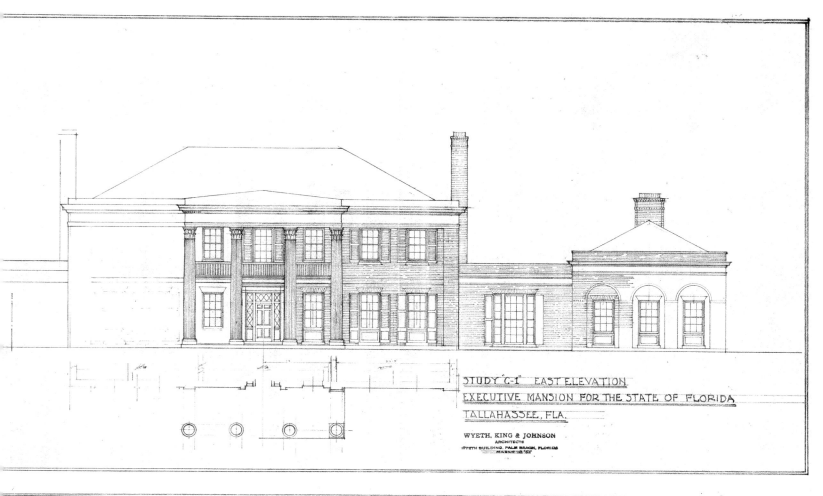

STUDY "C-1" EAST ELEVATION

EXECUTIVE MANSION FOR THE STATE OF FLORIDA

TALLAHASSEE, FLA.

WYETH, KING & JOHNSON
ARCHITECTS
WYETH BUILDING, PALM BEACH, FLORIDA
MARCH 18 '55

STUDY "C-2" EAST ELEVATION

EXECUTIVE MANSION FOR THE STATE OF FLORIDA

TALLAHASSEE, FLA.

WYETH, KING & JOHNSON
ARCHITECTS
WYETH BUILDING, PALM BEACH, FLORIDA
MARCH 18 '55

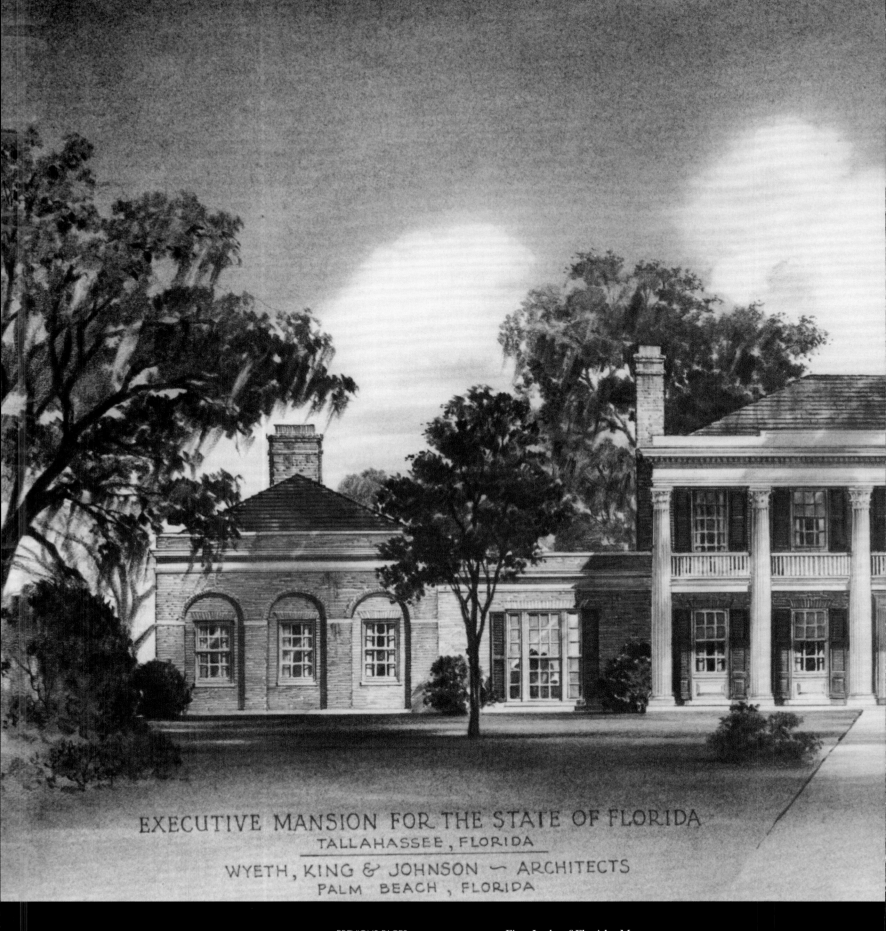

EXECUTIVE MANSION FOR THE STATE OF FLORIDA
TALLAHASSEE, FLORIDA

WYETH, KING & JOHNSON — ARCHITECTS
PALM BEACH, FLORIDA

PREVIOUS PAGES
Alternate roof and porch designs were studied but rejected because of expense.

First Lady of Florida, Mary Call Collins preferred this hipped roofed design, but Secretary of State Robert A. Gray insisted on the flat roof because of cost.

W. Mc Tammany, Del.
1955

further complicated by a restrictive budget and a legislative timetable that dictated that construction could not take more than three hundred days.[13] Contractor J. O. Carlisle of Tallahassee was chosen to build the structure through a competitive bidding process, and at the suggestion of Mrs. John H. Phipps, who served on the advisory committee, James Cougar, who had been the Curator of Colonial Williamsburg for seventeen years, agreed to be the interior decorator for the mansion.[14]

As plans were finalized, Marion Sims Wyeth developed the formal design for the building by taking advantage of the contour of the land. Approached from the east, the front of the house appears as a two-story Greek Revival central block with one-story wings that extend to the north and south. In truth, because the mansion is situated on the crest of the steep hill Wyeth noticed at the beginning of the job, he was able to add a third ground floor which was exposed on the western rear elevation. This western facade includes staff entrances and offices, a laundry, and elevator to the rooms above. But even with the basic form and volume problems solved, financial woes continued to plague the project. At one-point, air conditioning was only included in an alternate bid "so that it may be eliminated to cut costs if necessary." Governor Collins noted that the cost to air condition the mansion would be between $15,000 and $20,000.[15]

The style of the roof was also in contention, and the final design decision was made because of cost rather than aesthetics. Wyeth drew three elevations showing three different roof and pavilion designs. The first was a flat roof, the other two were hipped roofs of various heights with alternate pavilion designs and changes to the second-floor porch. In a 2005 interview, First Lady Mary Call Collins related that "she preferred the hipped roof design of the pavilions, but it was Captain Gray (Secretary of State Robert A. Gray) who insisted that the roofs be flat to avoid what he considered too great an expense."[16] In the end, the cheaper flat roofed design was chosen but the interior was air conditioned. Compromises had been made and in May 1955, the Legislature increased the building appropriation total to $290,000 to cover unexpected costs. Marion Sims Wyeth commented: "This is a public monument, not just a house. We've got to build something worthwhile."[17]

Throughout the building of the Governor's Mansion, Wyeth was praised for his attention to detail. At the main entrance, the two-story temple front, which is typical of Greek Revival-style structures, contains five bays with cast stone Corinthian columns and a second-floor balcony. The columns are similar to those at the Hermitage but have been changed slightly and are said to resemble the stylized leaves of the sago palm to give the house a Florida feel. The facade is symmetrical with double hung windows and shutters. The construction material is hollow clay tile covered with brick that was manufactured in Tennessee in the "Kingsport Hermitage Colonial style."[18] The interior contained hardwood floors laid in a Monticello block pattern and cypress paneling. Family rooms were on one side of the house with state rooms on the other. The *Tallahassee Democrat* praised the design and noted that the First Family will occupy a home that combines the spirit of the past with modern planning.[19]

Rhea Chiles, wife of Governor Lawton Chiles and first lady of Florida from 1991 to 1998, wrote that "four decades have attested to the genius of Wyeth's plan, the craftmanship of Carlisle's workers and the serene beauty of the Tallahassee local."[20] At age ninety-two, Wyeth commented on the project and the difficulty of pleasing so many parties, "It had to be formal and livable too. It was the hardest plan to conceive." But he remembered the job as one of his best. The State agreed and the Florida's Governor's Mansion was listed in the National Register of Historic Places in 2006.

CHAPTER THIRTEEN

A LIFE WELL LIVED

Wyeth typified the architect as trained artist and good citizen.

—Polly Anne Earl, Executive Director, Preservation Foundation
of Palm Beach from 1983–2004[14]

Architectural historians write about buildings and the role they play in shaping life. They study evolving form and style and discuss how materials and technology, as well as taste, stimulate change. Social historians remember the built environment but instead focus on personal stories that highlight individuals and events that help develop a community's sense of place. Architects and their work can be examined through both lenses. In a place like Palm Beach, which has been known for over one hundred years to attract wealth and extravagance, much has been written about grand homes and impressive public buildings. The architects themselves are sometimes forgotten while the names of famous clients stay connected to the buildings they commissioned. This has certainly been true of Marion Sims Wyeth, and one goal of this volume is to reconnect him to masterworks he designed. But Wyeth worked on more than the grand commissions presented here. Smaller works and renovations also filled his commission list and contributed to his success. Marion Sims Wyeth was a good citizen who helped build the community structure of Palm Beach contributing to the creation of the town where he lived and raised his family. It is this dual role in practicing architectural excellence while participating in civic life that elevates his career and warrants further remembrance.

When Marion Sims Wyeth and his wife, Eleanor, moved to Palm Beach in 1919 they had two daughters, an infant and a toddler, and the optimism of a young couple starting fresh. His first office was in the post office in West Palm Beach, but he soon moved that office to 207 Royal Palm Way in Palm Beach. The family first stayed with friends and then rented a house on Sea Breeze Avenue. They socialized with winter visitors and local professionals. Wyeth, with his Ivy League education, fit in well and was asked to join the exclusive Everglades Club in the spring of 1919. Eleanor played tennis and golf and was often pictured in the newspaper. Over time, two more children were born, another daughter and a son, and Marion's architectural practice prospered. They built their first home, Tre Fontaine, on what is now called Middle Road in 1924. Wyeth was asked to join the iconic Bath and Tennis Club and was a founding member of the Seminole Golf Club, as well as being its architect.

Built in 1925, the original Wyeth Building is now part of the First National/Wells Fargo Bank complex in Palm Beach.

Anecdotal tales paint a picture of the architect's life in Palm Beach during the early twentieth century. One of the stories that keeps recurring about Marion Sims Wyeth is that he was friendly with everyone, even his architectural competitors. Wyeth remembered, "Addison [Mizner] and I were friends all the time. We never had any fights or disputes and he used to consult me on proper procedure within the architectural profession which he knew nothing about. He was a great fellow."[2] Wyeth's son, Buz (Marion Sims Wyeth, Jr.), told of meeting Mizner when he was six years old and gives us a child's eye view of the famous architect. "Addison Mizner was rotund, obese, had a goat-tee. He had a Japanese houseboy and a pet monkey."[3] The monkey bit Buz. Historian Donald Curl noted that, "Wyeth was more of a friend than rival to the other early architects … and created character on street after street."[4]

As the number of commissions increased, Wyeth built his own office on South County Road. It could easily be overlooked today, as it is now incorporated into the streetscape of a much larger complex, the First National Bank/Wells Fargo building. Designed in 1925, Wyeth used all the skill and knowledge he had acquired completing the Golf View Road Development Company project and traveling to Spain to build his own three-story Mediterranean Revival–style office building. The Wyeth Building, as it was called, was mixed use. The exterior had all the grandeur of applied ornamentation but on a smaller scale than the houses. Tile, an engaged pilaster, a wrought iron grill, and a balcony over the street are all displayed. The roof was red tile. The brackets at the roof juncture add another Mediterranean detail. A Spanish-style bay window on the first floor opened up the interior for prime retail space. The Charles G. V. Clark Antiques and decorating business was the first tenant. The floorplan shows a small patio beyond the storefront. Mrs. Clark who combined her book shop with the decorating firm said she would use the patio for book discussions and tea. The doorway to the south of the window was originally

The first tenant in the Wyeth Building storefront was Burnet-Clark Ltd., an antique and decorating business. Wyeth's architectural office was on the second floor.

Eleanor Wyeth with her son, Buz (Marion Sims Wyeth, Jr.), at the Everglades Club.

BELOW
Marion and Eleanor Wyeth at the Bath and Tennis Club during the 1920s.

Board of Directors meeting at the Society of the Four Arts in 1946. Wyeth, who served as President from 1954–1961, is standing in the back on the far left.

arched and led up steps with tile risers to Wyeth's second floor architectural office and draughting room. The third floor had a small apartment for architectural staff.

It is important to note that the business relationships in Marion Sims Wyeth's architectural firm changed over time. It was founded in 1919 as Marion Sims Wyeth, Architect, Palm Beach, but Wyeth always had an informal association with his friend Frederic Rhinelander King in New York. Many of the early architectural blocks on the drawings contain the New York address: 52 Vanderbilt Avenue. The two men formalized their partnership in 1932 with the formation of Wyeth & King, Architects, New York and Palm Beach. In a telephone interview in 2005, Jonathan King, Frederic's son, said that the men were good friends and always known as "Uncle Freddie" and "Uncle Marion" to the children. "The firm divided the commissions with King doing everything north of the Carolina border and Wyeth doing everything south."[5] William Royster Johnson joined the business as a draftsman in 1925 and became a partner in 1944, making the business Wyeth, King & Johnson, Architects.

The Palm Beach Art Jury, which was the precursor to today's Architectural Review Commission (ARCM) was formed during the 1920s to review plans for "the express purpose of protecting property owners and the beauty of Palm Beach"[6] Wyeth served on the board with, among others, architects Addison Mizner and Maurice Fatio. Architect John Stetson later wrote about his experience as a temporary member of the Jury:

238

This group of men found it very uncomfortable at times because of the necessity of making decisions regarding poor design and in connection with zoning problems. Mr. Wyeth had a way of making insurmountable problems seem trivial. To me, a neophyte in the profession, he showed more than necessary interest in making my lot as important to the group as that of established members of the profession. Even with the high station he reached professionally and socially, he remains a humble man utterly interested in the problems of his neighbor and competitor.[7]

Besides working on the Art Jury, Wyeth was elected president of Palm Beach's Society of the Four Arts from 1954–56 with a second term from 1956–61.[8] Previously he had served on the board of directors. During this period, he was building the Florida Governor's Mansion in Tallahassee and became friendly with Governor Thomas LeRoy Collins. Collins came to the Four Arts on February 22, 1956, to lecture on the subject, "Florida Has the Green Light." As noted in the *Palm Beach Post*, the governor only appeared because of his friendship with Marion Sims Wyeth.[9] Wyeth was a member of the Palm Beach Civic Association and became a director of Good Samaritan Hospital, his first big commission. In 1928, Eleanor Wyeth was an organizing member of the Palm Beach Garden Club and was elected president of the auxiliary of Good Samaritan Hospital in 1955. The *Palm Beach Post* praised the couple with an article entitled, "Mr. and Mrs. Marion Sims Wyeth, Both Organization Leaders."[10]

Palm Beach like other communities revolves around its institutions. Schools and churches are two of the most important and Wyeth put his stamp on both. The Palm Beach Day Academy was started in 1921 as two separate schools, one for boys and one for girls. They merged in 1930, forming the Palm Beach Private School.

Palm Beach Private School, 1931.

Wyeth designed their new building in 1931. The *Palm Beach Post* reported that, "The building is of a simple, modern design, and will house both the boys' and girls' division on separate floors."[11] Wyeth's children attended for part of their education.

Wyeth made major contributions to the campus of the Episcopal Church of Bethesda-by-the-Sea, which was founded in 1889 and is the oldest church in Palm Beach. The present sanctuary, which is the congregation's third building, was designed by the firm Hiss and Weeks in the Gothic Revival style. The cornerstone was laid in 1925 and the first service was held in 1927. Wyeth's initial addition to church property happened in 1929, quite by chance, when the church bought one of Marion's Spanish courtyard houses to be used as the Rectory. A member of the congregation, Wyeth was hired in 1955 to design a much-needed parish hall (sometimes called the guild hall) to be built north of the main sanctuary. This new two-story building had eighteen classrooms for the church school, an updated kitchen and an auditorium that could seat three hundred and fifty people. His final addition to Bethesda-by-the-Sea was the columbarium where he and Eleanor eventually were buried. Designed in 1962 to complement the Gothic style of the main sanctuary, the structure could not be built until 1973, when the Town of Palm Beach Town Council gave permission to construct a "place of burial" on the island. The church dedicated the original three hundred niches in 1974 and the structure has since been expanded.[12]

Marion Sims Wyeth received one of the greatest tributes to his career in 1954 when he became the first member of the Florida South Chapter of the AIA to become elected as a fellow of the American Institute of Architects. That year he was one of only twenty-one architects throughout the country to be honored. The letters of support sent to the Jury of Fellows are illuminating and tell us a lot about Wyeth the man. Philip L. Goodwin, who with Edward Durell Stone designed the

Sketch by William Johnson of the Episcopal Church of Bethesda-by-the-Sea with the 1955 addition.

The columbarium at Bethesda-by-the-Sea was designed in 1962 but did not receive permission for construction from the Town of Palm Beach until 1973. Marion Sims Wyeth was buried here in 1982.

241

Museum of Modern Art (1938–39) in New York, had studied with Wyeth in Paris and wrote, "All the work Wyeth has done is intelligently planned and carefully executed."[13] L. Phillips Clarke designed the Palm Beach Town Hall when he was with the firm Harvey and Clarke. He wrote, "In 1919, I first met Mr. Wyeth, and worked for him for the latter part of that year. During World War II, I was in partnership with Mr. Wyeth doing architectural and engineering work for the Armed Forces." Clarke concluded his letter with a statement of high praise. "I believe Mr. Wyeth's ethics and fair dealings with owners, contractors and members of the profession are beyond reproach."[14] John L. Volk, another of Palm Beach's first-generation master architects, met Wyeth in 1930 and wrote, "He is held in high esteem as a man of great character and integrity, not only by myself, but by everyone in this community."[15] Wyeth was pleased with the honor and recalled with pride the celebratory dinner that took place in Boston, Massachusetts, in June 1954. He only had one disappointment. Mies Van der Rohe, who was also elected that year was at the Wyeths' table, and Marion remembered that Mies would not speak to anyone. "He was very high hat … a pretty snooty fellow."[16]

In 1981, the Palm Beach Chapter of the AIA honored Marion Sims Wyeth once again as the designer of "Architecture that has Stood the Test of Time." The dinner was at the Breakers Hotel. Although we have no transcript of the speeches made that night, the architecture that was highlighted was undoubtedly what I have emphasized in this book. Wyeth had started his Palm Beach career at the beginning of the boom times of the 1920s, and sixty years later it was obvious that his contributions had beautified the town where he lived as well as places around the state of Florida and the nation.

When Marion Sims Wyeth passed away in 1982, at the age of ninety-two, there were many tributes and remembrances. One warm and personal memory came more recently when the Preservation Foundation of Palm Beach recorded an oral history in 2017 with Mr. and Mrs. Henry Barkhousen, Wyeth's son-in-law Henry and his daughter Alice. Henry was articulate and generous. "Everybody liked him and appreciated him, above all he was really a distinguished man, you know, he carried himself that way professionally, very dignified and even though he had a great sense of humor, he was a gentleman of the old school."[17]

END NOTES

CHAPTER ONE

1 Polly Earl, "Early Architect's Remarkable Legacy Still Graces Palm Beach," *Palm Beach Daily News*, May 14, 1999,1.
2 Christine Davis, "Palm Beach's First Generation of Architects: Marion Sims Wyeth: Quiet, subdued and rational," *Palm Beach Post*, January 22, 2006.
3 "J. Marion Sims," *Encyclopedia of Alabama*, http://www.encyclopediaofalabama.org Accessed June 2020. For information on John Allan Wyeth see file on Wyeth Family at the Preservation of Palm Beach.
4 Application to Lawrenceville, note on file at the Preservation Foundation of Palm Beach, 1903.
5 *Princeton Alumni Weekly*. On file at the Preservation Foundation of Palm Beach. No date.
6 Handwritten notes on file at the Preservation Foundation of Palm Beach. No date. Also see Carolyn S. Denton, "Phone Interview with Buz Wyeth," November 7, 2002. On file at the Preservation Foundation of Beach. "Buz" is Marion Sims Wyeth, Jr., the architect's son. The prizes Wyeth won were the Prix Jean LeClerc in 1913 and the Deuxieme Prix Rougevin in 1914.
7 Marion Sims Wyeth, "Journal 1914–1915" Incomplete. On file at the Preservation Foundation of Palm Beach. For earthquake information see "American Officials Aid," *St. Louis Post-Dispatch*. St. Louis, Missouri, January 15, 1915.
8 *Palm Beach Daily News*, February 21, 1977.
9 "Eleanor Orr to Wed Marion Sims Wyeth," *Chicago Tribune*, October 26, 1915,1.
10 "Memorial," document on file at the Preservation Foundation of Palm Beach, no author, no date.
11 "Erection Good Samaritan Hospital Will be Commenced About July 1," *Palm Beach Post*, March 22, 1919, 1.
12 M. M. Cloutier, "Palm Beachers key in Good Samaritan's birth, growth," *Palm Beach Daily News*, June 25, 2000. See Also "Four thousand People Attend Great Washington Birthday Ball," *Palm Beach Post*, February 24, 1920, 1.
13 Jan Tuckwood, "Coronavirus Florida: How flu took down the Dodger brothers...and changed local health care," *Palm Beach Post*, April 6, 2020.
14 "Frank H. Clement to spend $175,000 in Developing Lake-to-Ocean Tract," *Palm Beach Post*, March 25, 1920, 1.

CHAPTER TWO

1 James R. Knott, "Designing Mar-a-Lago," *Fort Lauderdale News and Sun-Sentinel*. August 9, 1981. Although Wyeth wrote his recollections about this meeting and is quoted directly in Knott's article, the date 1920 in the article is incorrect and more likely was 1921. The Huttons were not married until July 7, 1920, and probably would not have been buying real estate together before that time. The plans for *Hogarcito*, are listed as Job # 42, 1921.
2 Nancy Rubin, *American Empress: The Life and Times of Marjorie Merriweather Post* (Lincoln, Nebraska: iUniverse, Inc, 2004), 111.
3 Ibid., 114.
4 "Hutton's Home in Palm Beach to Cost $35,000," *Palm Beach Post*, January 4, 1922. n.p.
5 Ibid.
6 E. F. Hutton to Marion Sims Wyeth, September 27,1923. *Marjorie Merriweather Post Collection*, Hillwood Estate, Museum and Garden, Washington, D.C.
7 E. F. Hutton to Marion Sims Wyeth, October 4, 1923. *Marjorie Merriweather Post Collection*, Hillwood Estate, Museum and Garden, Washington, D.C.
8 E. F. Hutton to Marion Sims Wyeth, January 12,1923. *Marjorie Merriweather Post Collection*, Hillwood Estate, Museum and Garden, Washington, D.C.
9 Marion Sims Wyeth to E.F. Hutton, December 22, 1923. *Marjorie Merriweather Post Collection*, Hillwood Estate, Museum and Garden, Washington, D.C.
10 *Palm Beach Daily News*, no date. On file at the Preservation Foundation of Palm Beach.

CHAPTPER THREE

1 E. F. Hutton to Marion Sims Wyeth, January 28, 1924. *Marjorie Merriweather Post Collection*, Hillwood Estate, Museum and Garden, Washington, D.C.
2 Marion Sims Wyeth to E. F. Hutton, June 26, 1922. *Marjorie Merriweather Post Collection*, Hillwood Estate, Museum and Garden, Washington, D.C.

3   E. F. Hutton to Marion Sims Wyeth, October 30, 1922. *Marjorie Merriweather Post Collection*, Hillwood Estate, Museum and Garden, Washington, D.C.

4   E. F. Hutton to Mrs. Jaffa, December 19, 1922. *Marjorie Merriweather Post Collection*, Hillwood Estate, Museum and Garden, Washington, D.C.

5   E. F. Hutton to Marion Sims Wyeth, December 19, 1922. *Marjorie Merriweather Post Collection*, Hillwood Estate, Museum and Garden, Washington, D.C.

6   Marion Sims Wyeth to E. F. Hutton, December 23, 1922. *Marjorie Merriweather Post Collection*, Hillwood Estate, Museum and Garden, Washington, D.C.

7   *Palm Beach Post*, April 27, 1923.

8   *Palm Beach Post*, April 17, 1923.

9   E. F. Hutton to Marion Sims Wyeth, January 28, 1924. *Marjorie Merriweather Post Collection*, Hillwood Estate, Museum and Garden, Washington, D.C.

10 "We Know Palm Beach," *Palm Beach Post*. September 30, 1925, 35.

11 "Charles E.F. McCann, 64; F. W. Woolworth Kin, Dies," *The Brooklyn Daily Eagle*, February 1, 1941, 9.

12 "G.H. Nicolai dies at Resort," *Palm Beach Post*, April 5, 1945.

13 "At the Everglades Club," *Palm Beach Post*. February 1, 1925, 12.

CHAPTER FOUR

1   "Philadelphia Fashionables are Really Resting in Palm Beach," *Philadelphia Inquirer*, March 30, 1924, 89.

2   Donald Curl, and the Boca Raton Historical Society, *The Boca Raton Resort & Club: Mizner's Inn* (Charleston, South Carolina: The History Press, 2008), 47.

3   "Ex-Brakeman Buys, Sells Utility Firms," *The Times*, Munster, Indiana, June 17,1951, 86.

4   Ibid. For Bradley Geist's comments see Curl, 45.

5   *Palm Beach Post*, April 4, 1925, 10.

6   Curl, 43.

7   Ibid., 48. See also "Geist Purchases $40,000,000 land at Boca Raton," *The Philadelphia Inquirer*, November 7, 1927,1.

8   Ibid., 59.

9   "Buildings are to be Erected in Boca Raton," September 9, 1930. Clipping on file at the Boca Raton Historical Society.

CHAPTER FIVE

1   *Palm Beach Daily News*, March 16, 1981.

2   F. Blair Reeves, Historic American Buildings Survey, HABS No. FLA-195, Mar-a-Lago. 1967. Mrs. Post's interest in anchoring the foundations of the house to the substratum is also discussed in Nancy Rubin, *American Empress: The Life and Times of Marjorie Merriweather Post* (Lincoln, Nebraska: iUniverse, Inc, 2004), 153.

3   "Stop Construction of Palm Beach Home," *Palm Beach Post*, March 6, 1926.

4   James R. Knott, "Designing Mar-a-Lago," *Fort Lauderdale News and Sun-Sentinel*, August 9, 1981.

5   Rubin, 153.

6   *Palm Beach Post*, May 5, 1925.

7   Over the years E. F. Hutton had five sailing yachts, cutters and schooners all named *Hussar*. This boat was number four and the first he owned with Marjorie Merriweather Post. It was built in 1923. The most famous of their yachts, which later was rechristened as *Sea Cloud*, was built in 1931. Kenneth Lisenbee, "Marjorie Merriweather Post: A Biography," http://www. PaulBowles.org 2009.

8   Knott.

9   Marion Sims Wyeth to E. F. Hutton, June 19, 1925. *Marjorie Merriweather Post Collection*, Hillwood Estate, Museum and Garden, Washington, D.C.

10 "Stop Construction of Palm Beach Home," *Palm Beach Post*, March 6, 1926.

11 Donald W. Curl, "Joseph Urban's Palm Beach Architecture," *The Florida Historical Quarterly* April, 1993, 441.

12 Knott.

13 Marion Sims Wyeth to E. F. Hutton, May 10, 1926. *Marjorie Merriweather Post Collection*, Hillwood Estate, Museum and Garden, Washington, D.C.

14 Allene Hatch, "Sea-to-Lake Dream Becomes Marjorie's Second PB Home," *Palm Beach Daily News*, September 9, 1983.

15 Marion Sims Wyeth to E .F. Hutton, September 10, 1926. *Marjorie Merriweather Post Collection*, Hillwood Estate, Museum and Garden, Washington, D.C.

16 Linda Saul, "Interview with Marion Sims Wyeth," on file at the Preservation Foundation of Palm Beach, 1977.

17 Curl, 442.

18 Rubin, 156-157.

19 Marion Sims Wyeth to Herbert A. May, July 7, 1961. *Marjorie Merriweather Post Collection*, Hillwood Estate, Museum and Garden, Washington, D.C.

20 Knott.

CHAPTER SIX

1 James W. Dodson, *The Story of Seminole* (Pebble Beach, California: Golf Lifestyles, Inc. and the Seminole Golf Club, 2007), 14.

2 "Plans for New Golf Club Announced by Winter Colony Men," *Palm Beach Post*, March 31, 1929. A clipping from the *New York Times* reports that while working on the Seminole, designer Donald Ross also laid out the course for Hutton's private "pitch and putt," on the grounds of Mar-a-Lago. "Private Golf Course: Broker Hutton Will Whack Some Pellets," *New York Times*, June 8, 1929. Since Donald Trump bought Mar-a-Lago in 1985, Donald Ross' tiny course has been replaced with turf and parking to accommodate an annual polo exhibition.

3 Nancy Rubin, *American Empress: The Life and Times of Marjorie Merriweather Post* (Lincoln, Nebraska: iUniverse, Inc, 2004), 150. This quote is also used in Dodson, 29.

4 For a full list of the Seminole Golf Club Founding Members see Dodson, 34.

5 "Seminole Golf Club Contract Let Friday; Work Starts June 1," *Palm Beach Post*, May 25, 1929.

6 Dodson, 44.

7 Dodson, 43.

8 "Seminole Golf Club Important Addition to Sport Facilities," *Palm Beach Post*, December 10, 1929.

9 Ibid.

10 "Ultra-Exclusive Seminole Golf Club Plays Host to 2020 Taylormade Driving Relief," *Ship Sticks* May 14, 2020. Accessed online July 2020. https://www.shipsticks.com.

CHAPTER SEVEN

1 R. W. Sexton, *Spanish Influence on American Architecture and Decoration* (New York: Brentano's Inc, 1927), 13. Sexton published photographs of five of Wyeth's 1924 houses in this book giving the young architect exposure and publicity.

2 *Palm Beach Daily News*, February 21, 1977.

3 "Malcolm Meacham Dies in Eleven-Story Plunge; Was Prominent Realtor," *Palm Beach Post*, March 14, 1929, 2.

4 "Meacham Property Bought by Bethesda for Use as Rectory," *Palm Beach Post*, April 13, 1929, 1.

5 Hillsborough County Planning Commission, "Oral History with Mr. and Mrs. Marion Sims Wyeth," 1980, On file at the Preservation Foundation of Palm Beach.

6 The Wyeths leased Tre Fontaine for parts of each winter season from 1932 to 1936. *Palm Beach Post*, December 20,1932, 3; November 16, 1933, 6; December 1, 1934, 3; April 17, 1935, 7; November 24, 1936, 3.

CHAPTER EIGHT

1 "Southern Colonial Architecture Makes a Palm Beach Appearance" *Palm Beach Post*, December 2, 1934, 5.

2 John de St. Jorre, *The Story of the Everglades Club* (Palm Beach: The Everglades Club, Inc., 2018), 180-183.

3 "Nearly Sixty Residences Built Last Summer," *Palm Beach Post*, November 22, 1936, 41.

4 "Palm Beach's Winter Residents Will find a Resort Beautiful on Their Arrival This Season," *Palm Beach Post*, August 19,1934, 1.

5 "Southern Colonial Architecture Makes a Palm Beach Appearance" *Palm Beach Post*, December 2, 1934. 5.

6 "Contract Awarded for Cudahy Home," *Palm Beach Post*, January 27, 1937, 9.

7 "Large house Will be Constructed for Mrs. Francis A. Shaughnessy," *Palm Beach Post*, July 3, 1938, 8.

8 "New Hospital Wing to be shown Sunday," *Palm Beach Post*, February 11, 1938, 11. The newspaper notes that Marion Sims Wyeth was the architect for the addition to the hospital that had been one of his first commissions in 1919.

CHAPTER NINE

1 Barbara Hoffstot, *Landmark Architecture of Palm Beach. Fourth Edition* (Pittsburgh, Pennsylvania: Pittsburgh History & Landmarks Foundation, 2019), xxii.

2 Elizabeth Wells, 'Home to Get Million-Dollar Face-Lift," *Palm Beach Daily News*, July 14, 1985, 12.

3 "Work Started on New Oceanfront Palm Beach Home; Strip Near Hutton's is Site

of New Residence; Contractor Brings Huge Crew from North to Construct Mansion Here," *Palm Beach Post*, January 19, 1927.

4   "J. P. Donahues Open New House at Palm Beach: Cielito Lindo Scene of Resort's Largest Party—Geraldine Farrar in Concert, *New York Evening Post*, February 21, 1928.

5   *Palm Beach Life*, January 11, 1949. Byron Simonson had been a draftsman and designer for both Addison Mizner and Maurice Fatio.

CHAPTER TEN

1   Marion Sims Wyeth to W. L. Baldwin, December 1, 1939. *Doris Duke Papers on the Shangri La Residence*, Doris Duke Charitable Foundation Historical Archives, David M. Rubenstein Rare Book & Manuscript Library, Duke University.

2   Louis Kemble, "World's Richest Girl Married in New York," *The Miami Herald*, February 14, 1935, 8.

3   Sallie Bingham, *The Silver Swan: In Search of Doris Duke* (New York: Farrar, Straus and Giroux, 2020), 103-104.

4   Ibid., 108.

5   "Extract from Letter Received from Mr. James H.R. Cromwell—from India," 1935. *Doris Duke Papers on the Shangri La Residence*. Architect Francis B. Blomfield worked with Edward Lutyens on the British government buildings in New Delhi.

6   Ibid., 2.

7   Alexandra Fatio, ed. *Maurice Fatio, Architect* (Stuart, Florida: Southeastern Printing, 1992), 93.

8   James Cromwell to Sam Kahanamoku, March 10, 1936. *Doris Duke Papers on the Shangri La residence.*

9   "Pays $100,000 for Property at Kaalawai," *Honolulu Star-Bulletin*, April 4, 1936, 1.

10 "Cromwells to alter Duke Estate Home," *The Courier-News*, Bridgewater, New Jersey, March 20, 1936, 1, and *Palm Beach Post*, August 30, 1936, 2.

11 "Doris Duke's Island Home Empty Dream," *Honolulu Star-Bulletin*, August 28, 1936, 1. See also "Cain Refuges to Reconsider Action on Pool," *Hawaii-Tribune-Herald*, August 29, 1936, 1, and "Does Hawaii Want to Keep Doris Duke Cromwell from Residence in Honolulu?" *Honolulu Advertiser*, August 29, 1936, 1. Duke built her seawall and swimming area on territorial land and it still has a path for public access.

12 Carolyn S. Denton, "Phone Interview with Buz Wyeth," November 7, 2002. Notes on file at the Preservation Foundation of Palm Beach, and "Marion Sims Wyeth Off For Honolulu," *Palm Beach Post*, February 7, 1937, 9.

13 Hillsborough County Planning Commission, "Oral History with Mr. and Mrs. Marion Sims Wyeth,"1980. Transcript on file at the Preservation Foundation of Palm Beach.

14 "Plenty of Room," *The Honolulu Advertiser*, August 13, 1937, 9.

15 Ibid.

16 "Doris Duke's Shangri La: Architecture, Landscape, and Islamic Art," Nasher Museum of Art at Duke University, Exhibition August 29–December 31, 2013.

17 Thomas Mellins and Donald Albrecht, eds. *Doris Duke's Shangri La: A House in Paradise* (New York: Skira Rizzoli Publications, Inc., 2012), 175-181.

18 Duke and her adviser, Mary Crane visited the site in 1938 and supplied Wyeth with detailed photographs of the Iranian building.

19 Bingham, 129.

20 Mieke ten Have, "A Rare Look Inside Doris Duke's Shangri La Home in Hawaii," *Vogue*. March 5, 2015. The name of the Pavilion is sometimes spelled Chihi Sutun although this spelling also references a building in Afghanistan which is not the inspiration for the "Playhouse."

CHAPTER ELEVEN

1   Plaque in the original entrance hall of the Norton Gallery and School of Art. Norton made a similar statement in 1940 when making his gift to the community "… for the education and pleasure of the public." "The Norton Gift," *Palm Beach Post*, March 31, 1940, 4.

2   R. E. Turpin, "New Art Institution Here Should Exert Wide Influence," *Palm Beach Post*, February 6, 1941, 2.

3   The Norton House at 253 Barcelona Drive, West Palm Beach, is now part of the Anne Norton House and Sculpture Garden. Anne Weaver Norton was the Ralph Norton's second wife and an accomplished sculptor. The site was listed in the National Register of Historic places in 1990.

4   Olivia Gazzam Morrish, *A History of the Society of the Four Arts: A Narrative of Significant Events from 1936 to 1983* (Palm Beach, Florida: Four Arts Publication, 1983), 114.

5   Ellen F. Roberts and Lesley A. Wolff, *Ralph Norton and his Museum* (West Palm Beach, Florida: Norton Museum of Art, 2019), 54.

6 Ibid.

7 Ibid., 55. The other two sculptors considered for the commission were Maxfield H. Kirk and Fred M. Torrey.

8 Gary Schwan, "The Curious Case of the Switched Statues," *Palm Beach Post*, July 24, 1985, 29.

9 Roberts and Wolff, 55.

10 Wm. Royster Johnson to *Palm Beach Post*, August 11, 1985. On file at the Norton Museum of Art, West Palm Beach, Florida, Archives.

11 Pam Parry: Senior Registrar, Norton Museum of Art, West Palm Beach, Florida.

12 R. E. Turpin, "Great Art Center Throws Open its Doors," *Palm Beach Post.* February 9, 1941, 2.

CHAPTER TWELVE

1 *Winter Haven Daily News Chief*, 15 April 1956, n.p.

2 U.S Census of 1950, retrieved from http://www.census.gov.

3 Peggy May, "A Place to Call Home," *Northwest Florida Daily News*, Fort Walton Beach, Florida (July 13, 1997), 1C.

4 Walter E. Keyes, director of the Florida State Improvement Commission to Governor Daniel McCarty, 23 February 1953, Florida State Archives.

5 Jean Houston Daniel, *Executive Mansions and Capitals* (New York: Country Beautiful for Putnam, 1969), np.

6 "Two Introduce House Protest of Mansion Site," *Tallahassee Democrat*, May 23, 1955, 1.

7 John Stenning, "Contemporary Design Preferred: Colonial Mansion Plan Brings Protest from Progressive Architects," *The Miami Herald*, June 19, 1955, 80.

8 Ellen J. Uguccioni, *First Families in Residence: Life at the Florida Governor's Mansion* (Palm City Florida: Boyd Brothers Inc. 2006), 43

9 John Stenning, "Size and Dignity Emphasized in New Executive Mansion," *The Miami Herald,* June 12, 1955, G1.

10 Rhea Chiles, ed. *700 North Adams Street* (Tallahassee, Florida: The Florida Governor's Mansion Foundation, 1997), 30

11 "Architectural Firm Engaged for Mansion," *Tallahassee Democrat*, February 8, 1955, 1; and "Palm Beach Firm to Design Mansion: Cabinet Wives 'to Advise,'" *Miami Herald*, February 9, 1955, 3.

12 Ibid.

13 "Size and Dignity Emphasized in New Executive Mansion," *Miami Herald*, June 12, 1955, 83.

14 United States Department of the Interior, Heritage Conservation and Recreation Service: "National Register of Historic Places, Registration Form," Florida Governor's Mansion, 700 North Adams Street, Tallahassee, Florida, January 9, 2006.

15 Stenning.

16 Uguccioni, 44-48.

17 "Governor's Mansion Cost Upped," *Miami Herald*, May11, 1955, 11.

18 Chiles, 31.

19 Joy Paisley, "First Family Will Occupy Home Combining Spirit of Past with Modern Planning," *Tallahassee Democrat*, September 18, 1955, 23.

20 Chiles, 35.

21 Ibid., 29.

CHAPTER THIRTEEN

1 Polly Earl, "Early Architect's Remarkable Legacy Still Graces Palm Beach," *Palm Beach Daily News*, May 14, 1999, 1.

2 Hillsborough County Planning Commission, "Oral History with Mr. and Mrs. Marion Sums Wyeth," 1980. On file at the Preservation Foundation of Palm Beach, 2.

3 Carolyn S. Denton, "Phone Interview with Buz Wyeth," November 7, 2002. On file at the Preservation Foundation of Beach.

4 Earl.

5 Carolyn S. Denton, "Phone Interview with Rev. Johnathon King," February 17, 2005. On file at the Preservation Foundation of Palm Beach.

6 "Art Jury Safeguards Property Owners in Palm beach Against Unartistic Building Erections," *Palm Beach Daily News*, no date. On file at the Historical Society of Palm Beach County.

7 John Stetson to Jury of Fellows, October 26, 1953. On file at the Preservation Foundation of Palm Beach.

8 Olivia Gazzam Morrish, *A History of the Society of the Four Arts: A Narrative of Significant Events from 1936 to 1983* (Palm Beach, Florida: Society of the Four Art 1983), Dedication, n.p.

9   "Governor Collins to Lecture Feb 22 Before Four Arts," *Palm Beach Post,* October 30, 1955, 23.

10 "Mr. and Mrs. Marion Sims Wyeth, Both Organization Leaders," *Palm Beach Post,* February 14, 1954.

11 "P. B. Private School Work Moves Ahead," *Palm Beach Post.* October 20, 1931, 3.

12 Kathryn E. Hall, *History of the Episcopal Church of Bethesda-by-the-Sea 1889-1989* (Palm Beach, Florida: The Episcopal Church of Bethesda-by-the-Sea, 1993), 59-60 and 99-100.

13 Philip L. Goodwin to Jury of Fellows, October 26, 1953. On file at the Preservation Foundation of Palm Beach.

14 L. Phillips Clarke to Jury of Fellows, October 21, 1953. On file at the Preservation Foundation of Palm Beach.

15 John L. Volk to Jury of Fellows, October 2, 1953. On file at the Preservation Foundation of Palm Beach.

16 Hillsborough County Planning Commission, 18.

17 Katherine Jacobs, "Oral History with Mr. and Mrs. Henry Barkhausen" 2017. On file at the Preservation Foundation of Palm Beach.

SELECTED BIBLIOGRAPHY

ARCHIVAL SOURCES

Boca Raton Historical Society and Museum, Boca Raton, Florida.
Doris Duke Foundation for Islamic Art, Archives, Honolulu, Hawaii.
Doris Duke Papers on the Shangri La Residence, Doris Duke Charitable Foundation Historical Archives, David M. Rubenstein Rare Book & Manuscript Library, Duke University, Durham, North Carolina.
Florida State Archives, Tallahassee, Florida.
Historical Society of Palm Beach County.
Marjorie Merriweather Post Collection, Hillwood Estate, Museum and Garden, Washington, D. C.
Norton Museum of Art, West Palm Beach, Florida.
Preservation Foundation of Palm Beach, Palm Beach, Florida.

BOOKS

Bingham, Sallie. *The Silver Swan: In Search of Doris Duke.* New York: Farrar, Straus and Giroux, 2020.
Bricker, Lauren Weiss. *The Mediterranean House in America.* New York: Abrams, 2008.
Chiles, Rhea, ed. *700 North Adams Street.* Tallahassee, Florida: The Florida Governor's Mansion Foundation, 1997.
Curl, Donald, and the Boca Raton Historical Society. *The Boca Raton Resort & Club: Mizner's Inn.* Charleston, South Carolina: The History Press, 2008.
Daniel, Jean Houston, *Executive Mansions and Capitals.* New York: Country Beautiful for Putnam, 1969.
De St. Jorre, John. *The Story of the Everglades Club.* Palm Beach: The Everglades Club, Inc. 2018.
Devine, Olympia. *Mar-a-Lago: From Ocean to Lake.* Palm Beach, Florida: Golden Lion Publishing for Mar-a-Lago Club, L.L.C., 2016.
Dodson, James. *The Story of Seminole.* Pebble Beach, California: Golf Lifestyles, Inc. and the Seminole Golf Club, 2007.
Dunlop, Beth. *Addison Mizner, Architect of Fantasy and Romance.* New York: Rizzoli International Publications, Inc., 2019.
Earl, Polly Anne. *Palm Beach: An Architecture Legacy.* New York: Rizzoli International Publications, Inc., 2002.
Fatio, Alexandra, ed. *Maurice Fatio, Architect.* Stuart, Florida: Southeastern Printing, 1992.
Hall, Kathryn E. *History of the Episcopal Church of Bethesda-by-the-Sea 1889-1989.* Palm Beach, Florida: The Episcopal Church of Bethesda-by-the-Sea, 1993.
Hoffstot, Barbara. *Landmark Architecture of Palm Beach.* Fourth Edition. Pittsburgh, Pennsylvania: Pittsburgh History & Landmarks Foundation, 2019.
Johnson, Shirley. *Palm Beach Houses.* New York: Rizzoli International Publications, Inc., 1991.
Labell, Shellie, Amanda Skier and Katherine Jacob, *Palm Beach, An Architectural Heritage: Stories in Preservation and Architecture.* New York: Rizzoli International Publications, Inc., 2018.
Mellins, Thomas, and Donald Albrecht, eds. *Doris Duke's Shangri La: A House in Paradise.* New York: Skira Rizzoli Publications, Inc., 2012.
Morrish, Olivia Gazzam. *A History of the Society of the Four Arts: A Narrative of Significant Events from 1936 to 1983.* Palm Beach, Florida: Society of the Four Arts, 1983.
Perkins, Stephen and James Caughman. *Addison Mizner: The Architect Whose Genius Defined Palm Beach.* Guilford, Connecticut: Lyons Press, 2018.
Roberts, Ellen F. and Lesley A. Wolff, *Ralph Norton and his Museum.* West Palm Beach, Florida: Norton Museum of Art, 2019.
Rubin, Nancy. *American Empress: The Life and Times of Marjorie Merriweather Post.* Lincoln, Nebraska: iUniverse, Inc., 2004.
Showalter, J. Camille. *The Many Mizners: California Clan Extraordinary.* Oakland, California: The Oakland Museum, 1978.
Standiford, Les. *Palm Beach, Mar-a-Lago and the Rise of America's Xanadu.* New York: Atlantic Monthly Press, 2019.
Uguccioni, Ellen J. *First Families in Residence: Life at the Florida Governor's Mansion.* Palm City Florida: Boyd Brothers Inc., 2006.

Curl, Donald W. "Joseph Urban's Palm Beach Architecture," *The Florida Historical Quarterly* (April 1993): 436-457.
    "The Florida Architecture of F. Burrall Hoffman, Jr., 1882-1980," *The Florida Historical Quarterly* (Spring 1998): 399-416.
Have, Mieke ten. "A Rare Look Inside Doris Duke's Shangri La Home in Hawaii," *Vogue,* (March 5, 2015).
Vickers, Raymond B. "Addison Mizner: Promoter in Paradise," *The Florida Historical Quarterly* (Spring 1997): 381-407.

The Brooklyn Daily Eagle, Brooklyn, New York.
Chicago Tribune, Chicago, Illinois.
Fort Lauderdale News and Sun-Sentinel, Fort Lauderdale, Florida.
Honolulu Star-Bulletin, Honolulu, Hawaii.
Miami Community Newspapers, Miami, Florida.
The Miami Herald, Miami, Florida.
New York Evening Post, New York, New York.
The New York Times, New York, New York.
Northwest Florida Daily News, Fort Walton Beach, Florida,
Palm Beach Daily News, Palm Beach, Florida.
Palm Beach Life, Palm Beach, Florida.
Palm Beach Post, West Palm Beach, Florida.
Philadelphia Inquirer, Philadelphia, Pennsylvania.
St. Louis Post-Dispatch, St. Louis, Missouri.
Tallahassee Democrat, Tallahassee, Florida.
Winter Haven Daily News Chief, Winter Haven, Florida.

Reeves, F. Blair. Historic American Buildings Survey, HABS No.FLA-195, Mar-a-Lago. 1967.
Research Atlantica, Inc. "Town of Palm Beach, Florida, Historic Sites Survey," Town of Palm Beach, Florida: Planning, Zoning and Building Department, 1997.
Rossin, Betsy. "The Essence of Wyeth," Savannah College of Art and Design, March 2017.
United States Department of the Interior, Heritage Conservation and Recreation Service: "National Register of Historic Places, Registration Form," Mar-a-Lago, 1000 South Ocean Boulevard, Palm Beach, Florida, December 23, 1980.
United States Department of the Interior, Heritage Conservation and Recreation Service: "National Register of Historic Places, Registration Form," Norton House, 253 Barcelona Road, West Palm Beach, Florida, June 20, 1990.
United States Department of the Interior, Heritage Conservation and Recreation Service: "National Register of Historic Places, Registration Form," Florida Governor's Mansion, 700 North Adams Street, Tallahassee, Florida, January 9, 2006.

"Doris Duke's Shangri La: Architecture, Landscape, and Islamic Art," Nasher Museum of Art at Duke University, Exhibition August 29–December 31, 2013. Accessed July 26, 2017.
J. Marion Sims, *Encyclopedia of Alabama,* http://www.encyclopediaofalabama.org, accessed June 2020.
Kettler, Sara. "Marjorie Merriweather Post & The History of Mar-a-Lago," http://www.biography.com/news/mar-a-lago-history, March 15, 2017 accessed May 25, 2018.
Lisenbee, Kenneth. "Marjorie Merriweather Post: A Biography," http://www.PaulBowles.org, 2009, accessed June 16, 2018.
"Ultra-Exclusive Seminole Golf Club Plays Host to 2020 Taylormade Driving Relief," Ship Sticks, May 14, 2020. Accessed online July 2020. https://www.shipsticks.com.
U.S. Census Bureau 1950 retrieved from http://www.census.gov.

ACKNOWLEDGMENTS

Writing about Marion Sims Wyeth, a prolific architect with a long career, was an arduous task that could not have been completed without the help and encouragement of many people. Amanda Skier, president of the Preservation Foundation of Palm Beach, showed great faith in me when she asked me to revive a project that my late friend Donald Curl had begun almost twenty years ago. Although Curl left no manuscript of his work, I sometimes ran across notes he had jotted in file folders, or an occasional email. I felt I was following in the footsteps of one of South Florida's great architectural historians.

The project began with the help of Marion Sims Wyeth's son-in-law Henry Barkhousen and his daughter Alice. They gave an insightful interview attesting to their early years in Palm Beach and Wyeth's character. Later I had the good fortune to hear from Wyeth's granddaughter Ellie Wyeth, who supplied the photograph of her grandparents at the Bath and Tennis Club.

At the foundation, archivist Shellie Labell got me started with initial research before she moved out of state. Katherine Jacob immediately stepped in, searching for images and everything else I needed. In a full day of joyful deliberation, Katie and Amanda collaborated with me on what illustrations to include in this book while mapping out a plan to commission new photographs. Their good taste is obvious from the results.

Carmel Brantley of Brantley Photography took many of the new photographs that add so much beauty to this text and show the breadth of Wyeth's work. From a preservation perspective her work helps provide a comparison between the past and present. Anita Selzer contributed her award-winning photograph of the statue *Diana* at the Norton Museum. I thank Anita for her friendship and am honored her artwork is included.

The photography of interior spaces could only have been completed with the generous permission of property owners. These include Jeffrey and Marsha Perelman, Thomas and Kristen Roberts, and Betsy and Paul Shiverick. The Reverend James Harlan, Rector at the Episcopal Church of Bethesda-by-the-Sea granted access to the Rectory, and Natalie and Tim Frank made arrangements to photograph Bienestar with former condominium president James Diack. The Seminole Club happily provided photographs for the project. Architect Kristen Kellogg, who had just completed the restoration of Southwood, was also kind to obtain permission to document the house and grounds. Jose Rodriquez shared a marvelous album of Southwood's historic images.

Palm Beach County historical institutions offered important assistance. Debi Murray, chief curator, and Rose Guerrero, research director, from the Historical Society of Palm Beach County supplied historic images for the book. Susan Gillis, curator of collections at the Boca Raton Historical Society and Museum, assisted with all things related to Clarence Geist. Scott Lese and Laura Ricardel of the Everglades Club helped with research of early Palm Beach history.

Archival research in facilities outside of Palm Beach County was complicated because of the Covid-19 pandemic in 2020. Early in my research I was able to visit the Hillwood Estate Museum & Garden in Washington, D. C. Abby Stambach, head of Archives & Special Collections, pulled boxes of documents, unsure of what might be useful. A small cache of letters between Wyeth and E. F. Hutton illuminated the seeds of their friendship, while giving rare insight into the building of Hogarcito, Mar-a-Lago and the development of Golf View Road. My sister Susan Phillips chauffeured me through Washington and cheered on my quest with love and support.

By the time arrangements were being finalized to fly to Hawaii to visit the Shangri La Museum of Islamic Art, Culture & Design, the trip became impossible because of Covid-19. Kristen Roth-Schrefer, Kristen Remington and Katrina Michelsen, all from the Doris Duke Charitable Foundation and Doris Duke Foundation for Islamic Art, answered questions and sent me to Elizabeth Dunn at the David M. Rubenstein Rare Book and Manuscript Library at Duke University in North Carolina. Elizabeth obtained permission to use historic photographs of Shangri La and went the extra mile, researching boxes and folders I could not access myself. I appreciate all of their help.

I first met Marie Penny while she was the archivist at the Norton Museum of Art. There she helped me understand the history of that important West Palm Beach institution. Later Marie became the archivist at the Preservation Foundation. She stepped into a half-finished project and seamlessly brought it to fruition. Marie uncovered documents no one had looked at in years and shared her knowledge of art and architecture. She acted as coordinator with Douglas Curran, graphic designer Abigail Sturges, and the talented staff at Rizzoli. Without her help and the expertise at Rizzoli this book would never have been finished.

Finally, two old friends made all the difference. Eugene Pandula understands architecture and preservation. We were lucky to work together for years while he served as the chairman of the Palm Beach Landmarks Commission. Gene listened to my ideas as the book developed and wrote a most generous foreword. Sandy Norman, a history professor at Florida Atlantic University and longtime business partner in Research Atlantica, Inc., edited the first draft, made suggestions and encouraged me to push ahead when my inevitable writer's block set in. Sandy's friendship kept me going. I appreciate all of her hard work.

INDEX

PHOTOGRAPHY CREDITS

1. © Brantley Photography
2-3: © Brantley Photography
4-5: © Brantley Photography
6-7: © Tim-Street Porter/OTTO
11: Preservation Foundation of Palm Beach Archives (PFPB)
12-13: PFPB
15: PFPB
16: PFPB
18-19: Historical Society of Palm Beach County
21: PFPB
23: PFPB
24: Historical Society of Palm Beach County
25: © Stephen Leek
26-27: © Stephen Leek
28: Photo by Frank Geisler, PFPB
29: © Brantley Photography
30: PFPB
31: Photo by Frank Geisler, PFPB
32: © Brantley Photography
33: Photo by Frank Geisler, PFPB
34: Photo by Frank Geisler, PFPB
35: © Brantley Photography
36: Photo by Frank Geisler, PFPB
37: © Brantley Photography
38-39: © Brantley Photography
40-41: Photo by Frank Geisler, PFPB
42: © Brantley Photography
44: PFPB
45: Photo by Frank Geisler, PFPB
46-47: © Brantley Photography
49: © Brantley Photography
50: PFPB
51: PFPB
52: PFPB
53: © Brantley Photography
54-55: © Brantley Photography
56: PFPB
57: © Brantley Photography
59: © Brantley Photography
60: Boca Raton Historical Society
61: Photo by Frank Geisler, PFPB
62: © Brantley Photography
63: PFPB
64: Photo by Frank Geisler, PFPB
65: © Brantley Photography
66: Boca Raton Historical Society
67: Boca Raton Historical Society
68: Photo by Frank Geisler, PFPB
69: © Brantley Photography
70: Photo by Frank Geisler, PFPB
71: © Brantley Photography
72: Photo by Frank Geisler, PFPB
73: © Brantley Photography
74: © Brantley Photography
75: © Brantley Photography
76-77: © Brantley Photography
78-79: Library of Congress
80-81: Library of Congress
82-83: Library of Congress

84-85: Library of Congress
86-87: Library of Congress
88: PFPB
89: Bert Morgan via Getty Images
91: State Archives of Florida
92-93: Library of Congress
95: PFPB
96: Seminole Golf Club
97: Historical Society of Palm Beach County
98-99: © Jonathan Cavalier
100-101: Historical Society of Palm Beach County
102-103: PFPB
104: Seminole Golf Club (E. F. Hutton portrait), PFPB (historic interior)
105: © Joann Dost, courtesy Seminole Golf Club
106-107: Historical Society of Palm Beach County
108-109: © Carlos Amoedo
111: Photo by Mattie Edwards Hewitt, PFPB
112-113: Photo by Mattie Edwards Hewitt, PFPB
114-115: © Brantley Photography
116-117: PFPB
118: Photo by Mattie Edwards Hewitt, PFPB
119: © Brantley Photography
120-121: © Brantley Photography
122-123: © Brantley Photography
124-125: PFPB
126-127: PFPB
128-129: © Brantley Photography
130-131: © Brantley Photography
133: © Brantley Photography
134: PFPB
135: © Brantley Photography
136 (top): PFPB
136 (bottom): © Brantley Photography
137: © Brantley Photography
138: Courtesy Jose Rodriguez
139: © Brantley Photography
140: Courtesy Jose Rodriguez
141: Photo by Samuel Gottscho, PFPB
142-143: © Brantley Photography
144: Sterling Morton Library
145: © Stephen Leek
146-47: © Stephen Leek
148: PFPB
149: © Stephen Leek
150-151: © Stephen Leek
152-153: Photo by Samuel Gottscho, PFPB
154-155: © Kim Sargent
156-157: Photo by Samuel Gottscho, PFPB
158-159: Photo by Samuel Gottscho, PFPB
161: © Brantley Photography
162: Photo by Samuel Gottscho, PFPB
163: © Brantley Photography
164-165: Photo by Samuel Gottscho, PFPB
166-167: © Brantley Photography
168: Courtesy Eugene Pandula
169: Kilo Content